You're a Failure, Get Over it!

How to Succeed by Deciding to Fail

Stephen Seal

Griffin Enterprises

Copyright © Stephen Seal 2013
10 9 8 7 6 5 4 3 2 1

First published in 2013 by Griffin Enterprises
5 Cian Lea
Swords
Co. Dublin
Ireland
www.Stephen-Seal.com

The right of Stephen Seal to be identified as the Author of this work has been asserted by him in accordance with Copyright, Designs and Patens Act 1988

All rights reserved. No part of this publication may be reproduced, stored in a retrieval system, or transmitted in any form or by any means, electronic, mechanical, photocopying, recording, or otherwise, without the prior permission of the publishers. Should you wish to contact the author or publisher for any reason please do so at author@stephen-seal.com.

ISBN-10: 0-9554180-2-X
ISBN-13: 978 0-9554180-2-0

Contents

PREFACE

CHAPTER 1: YOU ARE A FAILURE- GET OVER IT

Are You a Failure?	1
There are No Successful People	6
The Surest Way to Fail is Trying Not to Fail	8
The Key to Success is to Embrace Failure	9

CHAPTER 2: THE DEFINITION OF SUCCESS

What Others Say	12
The Lie of Happiness	15
The Real Definition of Success	18

CHAPTER 3: THE MOST IMPORTANT THING IN THE UNIVERSE THAT NEVER CHANGES

The Pendulum of Life	20
Life's Stabilising Fulcrum	22
Some Common Answers	23
The Danger of False Answers	26

CHAPTER 4: THE FULCRUM BECOMES A GUIDE

A Lost World	29
Some Temporary Solutions	30
The Measure of Success	32

CHAPTER 5: KNOW THY SELF

Not as Easy as it Sounds	39
The Three Components	40
Asking the Questions	43
Intrinsic and Extrinsic Work Patterns	45

CHAPTER 6: TAKE THE TIME TO THINK THINGS THROUGH THOROUGHLY

Autopilot or Manual	50
Think Before You Leap	54

CHAPTER 7: FIVE PRINCIPLES TO HELP YOU THINK THINGS THROUGH

THE FIRST PRINCIPLE: NEVER TRADE THE FUTURE FOR THE PRESENT	57
THE SECOND PRINCIPLE: TWO LOWERS NEVER TRUMP A HIGHER	60
THE THIRD PRINCIPLE: COMPROMISE WITH THE LEAST DISADVANTAGE TO YOUR KEY PURPOSE	62
THE FOURTH PRINCIPLE: IMPORTANCE TRUMPS URGENT EVERY TIME	64
PRINCIPLE FIVE: IMPORTANT TRUMPS ENJOYMENT EVERY TIME	65

CHAPTER 8: THE PROBLEM WITH NO

NO TO EVERY YES	68
THE TRUE MEANING OF BALANCE	70
FEARING NO	74
EMPATHY AND SYMPATHY	76
THE TABOO OF NO	79
YES AND NO GO TOGETHER	80
KNOWING WHEN	81

CHAPTER 9: HOW TO SAY NO!

STEP 1: EMPATHY	84
STEP 2: REASON	86
STEP 3: FAIRNESS	87
STEP 4: RESTORING CONTROL	88
PUTTING IT ALL TOGETHER	89

CHAPTER 10: SOME PRACTICAL TIPS

SAY NO…TO YOURSELF!	91
MURPHY LURKS EVERYWHERE	97
WATCH OUT FOR LOST DAYS	103

CHAPTER 11: AVOIDING THE TRAPS

TRAP NO. 1: SOCIALISING	105
TRAP NO. 2: FIRE FIGHTING	109
TRAP NO. 3: THE MISPLACED AND FORGOTTEN THINGS	114
TRAP NO. 4: THE 10 PERCENT RULE	118
TRAP NO. 5: PRACTICE FAILING	120

CHAPTER 12: DO THE RIGHT THING, THE HARD THING AND THE GREAT THING

DO THE RIGHT THING	125
DO THE HARD THING	128
DO THE GREAT THING	130

CHAPTER 13: PLOTTING THE TRAJECTORY TO SUCCESS

Where am I?   136
Where am I Going?   137
What Do I Need to Do to Get There?   139

CHAPTER 14: SOME FINAL THOUGHTS

Control vs Influence   143
A Little Bit of Fatalism Goes a Long Way   148
Enjoy Failing   151

Preface

There are numerous self-help books devoted to the topic of attaining success, so why did I write this one and, perhaps more importantly, why should you choose this one? These are good questions and the answer to both is the same. Having looked at many of the self-help books on the market today I found them to be deficient. They promise the moon and the stars, promise to turn your life around and solve all your problems and never deliver on these promises. Well this book is not like that. I cannot promise that after reading this book you will be rich, famous and powerful. I cannot promise that this book will give you a big house, two great children, a car in the garage and a white picket fence. All I can promise is that the principles laid out in this book will make a difference to you, what exactly that difference will be and how it will shape your life- well that is up to you.

Other self-help books take for granted the definition of success and that you want to achieve it. They believe that everyone wants to be a famous movie star or a billionaire entrepreneur, but this simply is not the case. As glamour magazines make women question their beauty, such self-help books make us question our value. If we are not the success these self-help books promise we should be, then we are failures and if there is one thing a self-help book is meant to prevent you from becoming, it's becoming a failure.

Well this self-help book is different. Not only do I encourage you to fail, but I encourage you to seek out failure, to purposely fail and then, once you have come to grips with being a failure, to be proud of that failure. I think part of the problem with our society, and why we are so unhappy, is not only that we set ourselves unrealistic expectations of success, but that we are ashamed of our failures. This has caused us to spend so much energy avoiding failure rather than following our dreams.

While some self-help books want you to accept your failures so that you can learn from them, never to repeat the mistakes again, in this book I will urge you to become a conscious failure, to remain a failure and, for the rest of your life, to continuously fail! You will have to read this book to see why this is important and why it will ultimately make you more successful.

While other self-help books urge you to copy the writer exactly, to follow their path and to be like them, in much the same way Mini-me, in the Austin Powers movies, was a smaller version of Dr Evil, that's not the approach of this book. Who really wants to walk in another person's shadow? Who wants to be a carbon copy of another person? So why try to emulate another person's success?

In this book I do not take for granted that I know what success means to you or that you should follow my path of success. The definition of success, while innately simply, is applied in as many ways as there are people on earth. Each and every one of us will achieve success in a different way and while some of the underlying principles may be the same, the end result is radically different. I urge you to think about your success carefully and to choose your own path. The examples I use in this book are not meant to be taken literally, you are not meant to follow them. They are there only to show you, in concrete terms, what the application of the principles this book encourages may look like.

Whenever I speak about my way of living and my success, you are not meant to take this as your way of living or your success. I use myself simply as an example of how some of these key principles have helped me to achieve success in my life, and while the principle will work for you, the exact route I have taken will not. You are you and you must be you, no matter what.

Before we move on I wish to say something about how the book is arranged. I believe that theory comes first, that really thinking about doing something before you do it is important. Therefore, the first couple of chapters of this book are dedicated to the underlying principles I believe we could all use to achieve success. This does not matter if you are a politician, a banker, a mom or a street sweeper. These principles will help you to experience more success and to ultimately achieve your goals.

As we move on, during the latter chapters in the book, I turn my focus to the practicalities of achieving your dreams. To the specific tools and techniques that can help you reach your gaols. These latter chapters are far more practical than the earlier ones-although they are meant, naturally, to be the application of the theory. With this in mind, let us delve right into it by looking at the important theories behind success and failure and what it really means to be successful.

Chapter 1: You are a Failure- Get Over It

Are You a Failure?

Often, when giving a seminar, I like to ask people the question: are you a failure? I have asked this question to thousands of people and am continually amazed at the passionate and emotive responses I receive. The vast majority of people will adamantly deny that they are failures. It would appear, from these responses, that to acknowledge our failure is to diminish our value.

Responses to this question often include a defensive element. For some reason people feel they need to justify their answer, they need to prove that they are not failures. The underlying thinking is that being a failure is bad while being successful is good. However, success is often associated with wealth, power and fame and yet very few of us can claim to have achieved in these areas. If we are not rich, powerful or famous then (so people's responses lead me to believe) we need to prove our worth and defend our value by affirming the success we are. We can do this by claiming to have a job, a family, to be happy or to help others. We can prove we are not failures by highlighting the good things in our lives, the things we have achieved (no matter how small).

The defence of our success often includes an element of comparison to those whom we think are "failures," those who have clearly failed in life. So for example, one may say "I am a successful person because I have a job, a wife, children and a nice home unlike other people who are unemployed, broke and divorced." If pressed, I find that most people will be able to name a person they think is a failure and who they believe is nothing like them. For example, they may say those who are in prison, or perhaps the homeless person who wanders the streets at night. These, I am told, are unsuccessful people because they have failed at the most important things in life; money, power, fame and happiness. If we have these things, so we think, then we are successful, without them we are failures.

How about you? When you read the heading above did you immediately think: "no, I am not a failure!" or did you pause for a moment to see what I would say before responding? When you read that most people think of themselves as successful people, does it make you feel more confident that you are part of this camp, one of the good people?

Before you answer, let me ask you another question: would you consider someone successful if they were continually failing? Is it possible to be a successful person and at the same time repeatedly fail? If someone was continually failing would we not call that person a failure? At the same time, if we label those who fail continuously failures, would we not be labelling the majority of us, including ourselves, for we are all failures?

You may object to my logic, you may be reluctant to label a person a failure lest you yourself be given such a designation. Before your objections progress too far let me ask whether or not it is simply our sense of political correctness, of politeness and positivity that prevents us from correctly designating those who continually fail; failures. What if I could demonstrate that all people are failures? That they don't do what they should do and that you yourself are a failure! Would this be an uncomfortable truth or a liberating realisation?

Perhaps you need some convincing, so let's pause for just a brief moment to explore my proposition. If we stop to think about it we realise that there is in fact a lot involved in being a successful person. Setting aside the popular mischaracterisations of success as money, power and fame, let me list (in no particular order) just some of the things most people would say they ought to do if they are to be successful in life:

- Do good deeds
- Donate some of your money to charity
- Exercise three times a week for an hour
- Eat a balanced diet
- Spend at least 2 hours a day with their spouse and children
- Speak to their family at least once a week
- Keep up regular contact with their friends
- Get a full 8 hours sleep every night
- Go to the dentist for a check-up every 6 months
- Save money regularly
- Manage and evaluate their pension every year
- Keep up to date with the news
- Spend time learning every week (for example: read a career-related publication such as a journal, magazine, or book)
- Spend some time volunteering in the community
- Keep your house, garden, car and office clean
- Investigate the important questions of life (why are we here, what is the meaning of it all?)
- Keep up to date with what does and does not cause cancer (avoid those things that do)
- Always listen to your children and partner
- Spend a few hours a week on a hobby
- Spend a few hours a day relaxing
- Watch some TV but not too much

- Attend to your personal hygiene (pluck your eye brows, shave, wax, and clean behind your ears)
- Take the dog for a walk
- Be on top of your work
- Invite people to dinner (your boss, your friends, the couple you meet at the PTA meeting)
- Keep up to date with popular culture (the latest singers, the salary of football players)
- Keep up to date with technology (the latest forms of communication, social media and the newest must-have gadget)
- Keep your carbon footprint down (recycle, change to energy efficient light-bulbs, switch off the TV at the wall, install that insulation, turn down the thermostat, don't boil more water than you need)
- Do the odd jobs (fix the draw, hang the picture, clean those curtains)
- Support your local economy by buying local

When we look at this long list of things we should be doing, it quickly becomes apparent that none of us are doing it all. Now it may be that I have listed items that you feel are not worth doing. Keep in mind, however, that the list I have given is hardly exhaustive or comprehensive. I am sure if you thought about it for a moment and wrote down your own list, you could easily add a few other items which you know you should do.

If you would like an interesting and challenging exercise then I would encourage you to develop your own list of what you think a successful person should do. Once you have a list similar to the one above, try to estimate how much time is spent on each item per week. For example:

- Sleep 8 hours a day (56 hrs.)
- Exercise 3 times a week for one hour (4.5 hrs. with prep and travel)

- Spend at least 2 hours with your children every day (14 hrs.)
- Stay in touch with family every week (3 hrs.)
- Walk the dog every day (2 hrs.)
- Practice good personal hygiene (4 hrs.)
- Relax for two hours a day (14 hrs.)
- Clean the house (4 hrs.)
- Keep the garden tidy (2 hrs.)
- Wash the car every week (1 hr.)
- Volunteer at a local charity (2 hrs.)
- Invite friends to dinner once a week (4 hrs.)
- Read every day (7 hrs.)
- Prepare and eat 3 healthy meals a day (1.5hrs a day, 10.5hrs a week)
- Do the shopping (4 hrs.)
- Keep on top of the odd jobs (2 hrs.)
- Dedicate 40 hours a week to work

Total number of hours spent per week on "good things": 179
Total hours available in the week: 168

No matter what activities you feel you need to do, it soon becomes apparent that there are not enough hours in the week to do everything you know you should be doing. It simply is not possible to do everything. Not only is there not enough time but there is also not enough money to do all that we need to do. If we are to put together a budget we soon realise that there is not enough money for most of us to do what we ought to do. Not enough money to eat the way we should, to keep our gardens, houses and cars in order, to support our children with the best things in life, to enjoy time with our friends, to take the holidays we want, to buy the clothes we would like or to support all the good causes in our community. Not only is there never enough time or money, but more than this, there is never enough energy and motivation to do all that needs to be done to be successful in everything. Every week, every month, every year we fail at something.

Is this to be our designation? Are we people who are unsuccessful, good at failing? What does it really mean to be successful, and is there a way that we can be successful without money, fame or power? It is these questions I want to explore during the course of this book. I am here to challenge your thinking, particularly when it comes to what it means to be a successful person and how it is that you can achieve this, because the truth is that there are no successful people who are not at the same time utter failures.

There are No Successful People

After trying so hard to be successful and speaking to thousands of people, I have come to realise that I am not alone. Everyone fails continuously to do what they believe should be done. There simply are no successful people. There is no one who is able to do everything they should be doing. There is no one who is the perfect mom, husband, best friend, boss, or employee. We, as a species, seem to be in a continual state of failure. We know what should be done, we continually acknowledge what must be done, and yet it is not possible for us to do and be all that we know we ought to be.

The problem becomes compounded by society's culture of pressurising us into being a good person. Ingrained within our psyche is a deep desire to be good people, to achieve and rise up to society's expectations of what good people do. We will resist any implication that we may not be good, successful people. We will fight tooth and nail any suggestion that we may not be the people we so very much want to be.

Let me challenge you if I may. If I asked you to list out all the things good people should do, how many of them do you think you do consistently? Would you say 40%, 60% or even as much as 80%? No matter which way you look at it, you know that there is still so much more you should be doing.

Often, when I discuss this with other people, I find that there are two ways of responding. There are some who acknowledge the problem. They know they should be doing more but feel unable to do so. As a result these people become unmotivated, despondent and downcast. There are others who, at the very suggestion that they may not be the people they know they ought to be, resist fervently the insinuation. They will say "no one can do everything" and because no one else is doing everything, they must be doing alright themselves. They compare themselves to others and other's failures and are soon able to justify their belief that they are good successful people.

Yet deep down inside there is an unsettled spirit within them. They know they should do more. Even if everyone around them is not doing all they ought to do, they know that they should be doing more. They know that good people have their lives in order, do everything they ought to be doing, accomplish what needs to be done. They want to be good people, want to be successful, but they don't really feel successful, they feel like failures!

The result is that although most people say they are good people, that they are doing everything they possible can do, they still feel inadequate. They feel like they are letting their friends, work colleagues, family and ultimately themselves down when they don't get around to doing everything they know they should do.

The truth of the matter, however, is that there are no good people. There is no one who is able to do everything that should be done. We all fail in some area or another. We are all bad people in some respect. Some are bad at house work, others at cooking some at exercise, others at keeping their car well maintained. Some struggle to keep in contact with friends and family, others struggle to keep up to date with their work. Some neglect their wives and others their tax returns. Everyone is bad at something, everyone has failures, everyone is a failure. There is no way of getting around this fact, you simply are not able to achieve everything you know you should achieve. You are a failure, so is everyone else...get over it.

The Surest Way to Fail is Trying Not to Fail

Before you get too discouraged and downhearted, let me lift your spirits by saying that there is hope. While I cannot guarantee that you will be able to do everything that needs to be done, I can, through the course of this book, help you to see clearly how to make the most of the one life you have been given. The next few chapters and pages will deal not only with the theoretical foundation necessary to make wise choices which will lead to overall success, but also with the practical steps you can take to ensure your life is well-spent on the things that really matter. So let us begin by considering the surest way to fail.

One of the surest ways I found to guarantee failure is to try not to fail. It sounds strange and almost contradictory, but those who try to avoid the inevitable failure that is a part of life, end up in a far worse situation than if they had simply chosen to manage failure. Let me explain further.

We know what we ought to be doing with our time, money and resources. Therefore, we often try as hard as we can to do everything. We often put all our energy into trying not to fail at a single part of our life. We spend our time, money and energy trying to do what we know should be done, but very soon we let someone down; our friends, our family, ourselves. We run out of time, money, energy and motivation and are simply unable to succeed. Since our resources are limited, the more we try, the more time, money and energy is misspent and wasted trying to avoid the inevitable. We don't have the resources to do everything and therefore using our resources to do everything is futile. The more we try not to fail the more we fail. We are so determined to be the people we know we ought to be, to do the things we know we should do, and so afraid that we are not going to be able to do it, that it soon becomes a self-fulfilling prophecy. The attempt to accomplish everything can only end in failure. There simply is no way out of this trap. We do not have the resources to do everything and our fear of failing at something leads us to spend our resources unwisely- resulting in even greater failure.

The general avoidance of failure is the surest way to ensure greater failure. As we try to accomplish everything we begin to fail at everything. We spread ourselves too thin, giving less resources to the most important things and as a result we end up being ineffective.

Yet what many do not understand is that the key to success is not to avoid failure but rather to embrace it.

The Key to Success is to Embrace Failure

The realisation that you are a failure, that you are not able to accomplish everything, is a liberating realisation. Once you come to grips with the fact that you are bound to fail, that it is an inevitability, a fact of life, written in the stars if you will, you soon rid yourself of the pressure to get everything right and become free to focus on what's important.

The key to success is not to avoid all failure, such an approach will only result in the mismanagement of your time, money and energy, ultimately ending in catastrophic failure in the most important areas of your life. In the same way as the desire to please everyone will ultimately result in someone being disappointed, the desire to avoid all failure will only end badly.

By embracing failure, coming to grips with its implication and consequences, you can free yourself from the pressures placed on you by those around you. By coming to grips with yourself as a failure you can begin to actively choose where to fail. By making a conscious decision to fail in one area of your life, you can make a conscious decision to succeed in another. If you embrace the concept of failure you embrace the freedom to choose where to fail. As a result you avoid the general failure experienced by those who try to achieve everything and embrace not only specific failures but also specific successes. This is the key to success.

The key to success is not avoiding failure. The key is to choose actively where to fail so that you may succeed elsewhere. By actively choosing to fail in some areas, you are actively choosing to succeed in others. So for example one may be failing at keeping their house clean but succeeding at spending time with their family. One may be failing at reading the latest booker prize winning author, but succeeding at keeping fit. You can fail at maintaining your car but succeed at keeping your friendships strong. By choosing where to fail, you choose where to succeed.

The key is not to avoid failure but to take control of it, to fail on your terms and to be proud of your failures because they represent your active choice of where to fail and where to succeed, rather than your surrender to the inevitable chaos that is life. I am proud of my many failures. My inability to maintain my garden has meant that I have been able to spend more time with my wife. My failing at reading more popular books has meant that I have had more time for my PhD. I have never watched a full episode of big brother or the X-factor but I have spent hours empowering others in my community and caring for those in need.

There is nothing wrong with failure if it frees you to succeed.

Chapter 2: The Definition of Success

What Others Say

I am often amazed at what is sold as success in this day and age. When I lead training programmes on the topic I sometimes ask the question "what is success?" Nine times out of ten I get the same two answers. The first, which will come as no surprise (although on closer inspection it is very surprising) is that success means having money, power or fame. The second is a little more thought through, although not thought through enough, and is that success means happiness.

These two understandings impact our daily lives. For example, when we are at a social gathering and we meet new people we are often asked what we do for a living. There is an underlying presumption (albeit completely false) that what you do for a living and who you are as a person are synonymous. To the question: what do you do? You may choose any number of answers you like. You may be a lawyer, a doctor, a policeperson or child care worker but whatever you answer it must conform to one of two types of activities if you wish to be valued by the asker. The first is that you earn a great deal of money, are powerful or are famous. This, for some reason or another, is very important to being successful. If you make a lot of money, drive a nice car, live in a big house and go on fancy holidays, you can hold your head up high when you tell someone what you do for a living.

The second type of activity has very little to do with money and more to do with whether or not society believes that your job or career path will contribute to the overall happiness of our community. If you don't make a lot of money doing your job, then you darn well better do something that "has meaning." If you work with vulnerable people, the elderly, children, people in need, then you are more than likely going to be liked by the strangers you meet at your Aunt May's 45th wedding anniversary. You may answer these strangers by telling them that you are a teacher, a fireman, a policeman or that you work for a charity. Any derivative of the aforementioned will be fine.

I have found that when I probe parents as to the types of careers they would like their children to follow, it always seems to be some derivative of these two basic activities. Parents want their children to make money, be powerful or contribute to the community. Modern parents, however, are very politically correct when it comes to their children. If their child does not want to follow a career that either makes them rich or supports the community, parents seem to know the answer they need to supply when telling others what their child does. Indeed the answer works if you yourself are involved in a career that does not conform to the goals of money and meaning. When a parent is asked what their children do, and they feel embarrassed to say, they will always include the words: "that's what makes them happy."

If you can't earn enough money or help enough people, then at least you can console yourself with the thought that what you are doing makes you happy. It appears, and this is only my assumption, that this answer "it makes you happy" will justify any career choice. You could be the administrator for a debt reclamation company on minimum wage calling pensioner after pensioner to reclaim their TV, but as long as it makes you happy no one will question your career choice!

Now I am not sure what it is about our society that causes people to automatically think that success and money go together. It may be the media, it may be the magazines and newspapers people read on their daily commute, or it may be that our friends and family are always talking about it. Certainly it seems to come up a lot in conversation. We are always talking about how much this costs and who paid what for which brand at which store. The pound and dollar sign are so common in our daily lives that it's only the number of zeros that shock us.

Even with all the houses, fast cars, fancy clothes and exotic trips, can we really say that the rich are more successful than the rest of us? It may appear that way at first, they may have amassed more possessions than the rest of us, but ultimately they will end up the same as everyone else. Their final resting place is, as ours will be, marked by a stone in the middle of a field. Many rich people will never be remembered, they will never make a lasting difference and their legacy will be nothing more than a few more zeros behind their bank balance. Does being rich automatically mean success?

Yet even though what I have told you is nothing new, that you have heard it all before, we still want those expensive suits, those Italian leather shoes and designer handbags. None of it will actually make a difference to who we are as people. Like a 5-year-old who gets an expensive present for Christmas and plays with it for a few hours only to cast it aside for something else, no amount of zeros and commas on a page will truly fulfil us.

The Lie of Happiness

Success is important and deep down inside we know that we can be successful, therefore it must be something that we can all possess, and since we can't all be rich (because then no one would be rich), and yet we can all be successful, success must be something available to all. For the last few decades as the world has struggled through modernism, post-modernism and now post-secularism, there seems to be one underlying principle that seems to be open for all, easy to obtain and universally available: happiness. Those who cannot be rich can still be happy and happiness, it would appear, has become our new god.

We love happiness, we worship it, follow it around, seek after it, spend our money on it, give our time to it, and devote our energy to obtaining it. It features in almost every commercial we see on TV. Buy these shoes and you will be happy, you will be glad you drank that drink, wore that perfume, drove that car. I have heard happiness justify all sorts of strange behaviour. Happiness has become the ultimate goal and the rules of the game are simple: do whatever makes you happy.

I find it particularly strange that we have substituted the word happiness for love. It appears that we want love because it will make us happy. This is the picture we get from all the romantic comedies we see in the cinema. As long as they are happy they love each other, but as soon as they are no longer happy they no longer love each other, until once again they realise that they are happiest when they love each other. I often ask people why they love their partner and the answer is almost always the same: because they make me happy.

In fact happiness seems to be a reason to get divorced. As long as we are happy with our wife or husband we remain with them, but when they no longer make us happy then it is time to seek happiness elsewhere. Love is no longer a word used to express support, commitment, stability and dedication. It is a word used to describe a state of happiness. If you are not happy you clearly can't be in love- so society would say.

It is amazing that this concept has gone so far that it has been used to justify illegal activities. Drug users will often cite their reason for the use of marijuana as: it makes them happy. And in our happy conscious society, I have heard so many people say that it is okay to smoke pot as long as it makes you happy and it does not hurt anyone. This is the basic principle of modern ethics: happiness. Do what you like; as long as you are happy and you don't hurt anyone it's all good. This is the message spread to our children: do whatever you can to make yourselves happy and do it now.

Even while reading this I am sure you are asking yourself what is wrong with that? We have been so indoctrinated with this concept that the mention of it no longer seems offensive. I don't believe this concept should go unchallenged in society and I don't believe it should go unchallenged in my life. Let's look closely at the definition of success and the role of happiness.

Let us say that success is being happy. What type of society do you think we would have if everyone did whatever would make them happiest. When the statement is phrased this way, the implications become clear. Obviously society could not work if everyone did whatever made them happy. Universal instant happiness is a sure way to universal permanent misery. If we all looked out for the well-being of number one, ourselves, very soon our society would collapse.

In fact our society is held together by those who are willing to give up their happiness for the well-being of others. History is filled with heroes who laid down their lives, who lived for the good of others and who experienced severe hardships, so that society as a whole might flourish. We think of the great many men and women serving as relief workers in the UN and other aid organisations trying to make a difference for the world. These men and women experience great hardship, they are often away from their families for months at a time, in very difficult conditions, sometimes putting their lives at risk and can hardly be called happy living in disaster areas where innocent men, women and children die from commonly curable diseases.

Now, it is true that ultimately such people (one would hope) receive a great deal of contentment in the knowledge that their sacrifice was, and is, for the benefit of others. This contentment may well be called happiness, but it is quite a different form of happiness to the one someone gets when they earn a large amount of money or buy a new outfit. It is more a sense of achievement, a contentment that comes from having done something worthwhile.

If we all sought only happiness, no one would find it. Let me ask you some questions. Do you think Nelson Mandela was happy in jail? What about Mother Teresa living in poverty, squalor and disease? Do you think Mahatma Ghandi was happy being beaten for standing on a white man's beach in South Africa or while starving during a hunger strike to save his country from civil war? Do you think he was happy when he was assassinated? No, of course you don't.

But do you think these people were successful? Of course you do!

The Real Definition of Success

As you can see, success and happiness are not synonymous. To be successful does not necessarily mean to be happy. In fact, often, it is the other way around. If one truly wants success, often sacrifice and hardship follow. Yet success is possible if we can clearly understand what we mean when we speak of success.

To me the definition of success is simple; success means simply to reach your goals. Success has nothing to do with how much money you have in the bank or how happy you are in life. To be successful means that you have reached your goal. Let me tell you a story to illustrate the point further.

I knew a man when I was growing up, I will call him James. His whole life he only wanted one thing: to save lives. He thought that if he could save lives then his life would be worth-while. Since he was bright and did well at school, he got into medical school. He went to university for 6 years and became a doctor. He spent the next few years specialising in paediatric surgery moving into paediatric cosmetic surgery to help children who have experienced severe burns. He was so good at this that he soon went on to cosmetic surgery for adults and after a few years opened his own private practice as a plastic surgeon for the rich. He drives a nice car, has a big house, married a beautiful woman and had two wonderful children. He is happy.

My question, however, is as follows: is he successful?

While many may answer, yes, of course he is successful. He is wealthy and is very happy, I would argue that while he may be happy and have a lot of money, he has failed to reach his life's goal. He no longer saves lives but instead spends his days making people look beautiful so that they might feel better about themselves. Just because he has money and happiness, does not automatically mean he is successful. Had James set out to make money and be happy then yes, he would by all accounts have reached his goals and therefore he would be successful, but this was not what he set out to do.

What about you? Would you consider yourself rich or even happy? Did you pick up this book because you believed it would make you rich and happy when the cover really spoke of helping you become more successful? Do you even know what success really means and especially what it means to you? If I asked you; what does success mean, would you reply "happiness?" If this is your reply, you need look no further. Happiness is within your grasp. Simply be happy, take a pill, drink a drink, smoke something, whatever makes you happy. Then, if happiness is your measure of success, you would have reached your goal and you would be happy- today, right now! This may be a temporary happiness and tomorrow you may no longer be happy, but don't despair for tomorrow you can take another pill, drink another drink and smoke another joint.

However, if you want contentment, if you want a lasting sense of accomplishment, a sense of achievement that lasts longer than simply a few hours then read on. I cannot promise that this will be easy or guarantee that you will achieve it, this is not that kind of self-help book. But I can promise that you will have a better chance at success and that you will be better off for trying if you follow the principles I lay out in this book.

Chapter 3: The Most Important Thing in the Universe That Never Changes

The Pendulum of Life

Grandfather clocks are amazing. They are imposing, carved out of beautiful wood and bring a sense of elegance to any room. One of the most fascinating parts of a grandfather clock is the pendulum. When I was a young child I could spend ages watching the pendulum swing. I was mesmerised by its movement, its hypnotic back and forth, back and forth. I always wondered how it kept swinging and how it was that the clock was able to harness its rhythm to keep track of time.

When I was about 15 years old we learnt about pendulums in science class. I will never forget an experiment we did in class one day in which the teacher tied six pendulums, each a different length, to a single piece of string. As she moved the string back and forth she was able to get each pendulum to swing at different intervals, each corresponding to the length of the string it was tied to.

While the actual pendulum may swing back and forth; a key component is the fulcrum. The fulcrum is the stationary point to which the pendulum is attached. It is always a fixed point. If the pendulum was not attached to this fixed point, it would not be able to continue its rhythm. Because of the fulcrum, whenever someone pulls the weight back and lets it go, the pendulum swings back and forth. Without this fixed point the pendulum would fly randomly in any direction. It would not swing back or continue its rhythm.

Life is a little like that. We all experience the swings of life. Sometimes we are feeling good and on top of the world, other times we feel awful and down in the dumps. Our lives swing back and forth regularly. It is believed that approximately every two weeks you will experience some form of crisis in your life. This may be as minor as a speeding fine, or losing your cell phone, or it may be quite serious, such as the death of a loved one or losing your job. It is simply a fact of life that we all experience these types of crises. But the pendulum should swing back, life should return to normal.

For this to happen there needs to be a fixed point around which your life centres; some point that never changes, that acts as the anchor to life's storms, the ups and downs of daily living. Without this fixed point (this fulcrum) your life may begin to swing endlessly from crisis to crisis, instead of back to normality. In such situations there does not seem to be a state of "normality," the regular, balanced, successful life we all seek. Rather there seems to be nothing but trouble- crisis after crisis.

I am sure you know someone who lives like that. Their life just never seems to be calm, they never seem to be on top of things, they are always trying to juggle one crisis after another. You yourself may be experiencing this. If this is the case, contentment is difficult to find, the regular enjoyment of life- that most of us experience on most days- seems to elude you and you are left with worry and anxiety. Your life does not need to follow this pattern, you do not need to live this way. There is a solution, there is hope.

Life's Stabilising Fulcrum

Just as that pendulum swings from one extreme to the next, because its fulcrum holds it in balance, your life needs a fixed point, a fulcrum to hold it in balance. You need to build your life on a solid, firm foundation that is fixed, stationary and never changes. Something that you can rely on, that you can fall back on. This will give your life balance, meaning and direction and will act as the anchor to ensure long-term success as your life swings between normality and crisis.

But how do you find such a thing? What is the foundation upon which you need to anchor your life? There are so many options to choose from; money, power, family, happiness, career, health, personal achievement, fame, material possessions, religion, the list goes on and on. What to choose and how to decide?

The answer, you may be surprised to learn, is actually quite simple. If you want to choose one principle, or guiding foundation on which to build your life, you need only answer one question: What is the most important thing in the universe that never changes? Answer this question and you will instantly know what to build your life upon, what to cling to in times of crises, so that you will be sure to return to a regular, long-term successful life.

To answer this question, you need to consider two things. The first is the principle of importance. Your life should be rooted in something of fundamental importance. There are so many people who build their life on unimportant things; things like appearance, clothes, the latest gadget, etc. They devote themselves to these things, spending their time, money and energy on them. They live for the latest movie, the newest fashion fad, the next football game. While this may bring them an incredible amount of enjoyment, ultimately it is of no value and they will find that they have wasted their lives on superficial things with nothing to show for it in the long-term. These are simply temporary distractions that cannot ultimately lead to experiencing true success.

The second important principle is that of permanence. A great many people spend their time, money, and energy on things that simply don't last. For example they spend thousands on their appearance and hours in front of the mirror. Others dedicate all their time and effort into careers that inevitably come to an end and when they retire they have nothing to show for it save for a small pension and a gold watch. If the pendulum is to swing back, if there is something in your life anchoring you, grounding you, so that you do not come undone whenever a crisis comes your way, you must ground your life in something that never changes, something that will remain with you throughout your whole life.

Some Common Answers

The question I am posing seems to be cryptic, mystical and complicated. Finding an answer that matches these criteria can seem difficult. However, once you find this answer you will be amazed at how obvious it was and how powerful this simple principle can be in helping to ground your life and establish your understanding of long-term success. Let me deal with some common answers.

As I have already mentioned, many people believe that the answer to this question is happiness. They feel that happiness is very important and that it is a principle on which to build their life. After all, they think, if one is not happy what is the point of living life? I have already discussed this philosophy and shown that true happiness is not something that comes as a goal in itself but is something that comes as the result of reaching a far greater goal, the term contentment is perhaps more appropriate.

The problem with happiness is that it is firstly not universally important and secondly it is subject to change. While happiness may be important to you, it ultimately has no real, long-term, lasting significance to the world you live in. Being happy today is no guarantee that you will be happy tomorrow and your happiness is no guarantee that those around you will be happy. As a result you will find that the constant desire to be happy is self-defeating. The more you try to become happy the more you focus on yourself at the expense of others. Sooner or later you reject, hurt and lose the people who make you happy and as a result you end up unhappy.

Secondly, happiness is not something that does not change. What makes you happy today may not make you happy tomorrow. If you build your life on something which makes you happy today, it is no guarantee that you will be happy tomorrow. Today you may love your job, but tomorrow you may hate it. Today you may love your freedom and the joy of being single, tomorrow you may love your children and your family ties. Of course you can always re-evaluate what makes you happy. However, in times of crisis, to depend on something that changes so radically as happiness, is like trying to cross a bridge made out of spaghetti; it will bend and sway and ultimately let you down. While happiness may at first appear to be a worthy goal, and it is certainly sold to as us such by the media, our family, friends and teachers; on closer inspection we find it fickle, fragile and unreliable.

Another common response is family, friends and relationships. This too, at first, appears to conform to both principles of universal significance and immovability. After all, you may say, what could be more important than my family. Here one may be right. Family is very important. It is the life blood of our society, the source of much happiness (and trauma) and the fundamental building block of a successful community. Yet family is anything but unchanging.

For a couple of years I managed a day care centre for senior citizens. The one lesson I learnt was that we will all die alone. I know this sounds sad but it is the truth. We may be surrounded by friends, family and loved ones now, but ultimately we will all face death alone. In the vast majority of cases one spouse dies years before their partner, leaving the other to face the rest of their life alone. Children grow up, leave home and move away. They find their own partners, have children and start new families. It is a sad fact, and one that needs to be rectified, that in the western world, the old are pushed aside, carted off to the local old age home to live their last few years alone.

Families simply don't stay the same. Take a look around you, how many broken families do you know? Divorce is on the increase, those who once promised to spend the rest of their lives with their partners have broken that promise. In divorce, one or both partners are left to face the dissolution of the marriage alone. In other families, children have rebelled or been pushed away by their parents leaving the family broken and desolate.

If you come from a family that is still intact, that still loves each other and is still together, then you can be very grateful. Take comfort in this fact and enjoy your family. Work hard to build and maintain strong healthy bonds. But be careful about thinking that it will always be this way. When we close our eyes at that final movement in life, no one will be with us, we will face the final curtain alone.

The Danger of False Answers

Before I move on, let me draw your attention to two examples where a crisis in the family can cause a life to halt and stand still. One such example is the terrible tragedy of the death of a child. There truly is nothing more painful for someone to experience than the death of their child. It is unnatural and incredibly traumatic for parents to bury their children. However, it does happen. In a healthy situation, a family with strong relationships, the grieving process, while difficult, will last about 18 months. During this time the family will experience extreme sadness as they come to grips with the situation.

However, in many cases people build their whole identities on their children. They devote their whole lives to their children and live vicariously through their sons and daughters. In these cases, the death of a child can be so traumatic that the parent never recovers. They are unable to continue the normal functions of life, unable to sustain their marriage, their job, their relationships with other friends and family. Their life grinds to a standstill and in extreme cases comes to a traumatic and final halt.

While a parent will never fully recover from the death of a child, if the relationship is healthy and they have not built their entire identity on that child, they can recover to such an extent that they can continue to function normally. They can continue to enjoy their marriage and other relationships, hold down a job and keep on top of life, they can still achieve their goals and while they never forget their child, or hurt at the thought of their loss, the pendulum is able to swing back to normality and they are able to carry on.

Children, however, for a far more common reason than death will ultimately leave their parents. When a child reaches a certain age they grow up, get a job, meet a partner and leave home. This is the natural cycle of life. Children grow up, they get jobs, get married and start their own lives. However, when a parent has built their whole life around their children it is possible at this point to get something known commonly as "empty nest" syndrome. This is a form of mild depression and sadness which often affects the mother, but can affect the father as well. Depending on their relationship with their children, this syndrome can be quite serious. Where unhealthy relationships exist, and a parent's identity and sense of purpose is solely based on raising children, losing them to the natural cycle of life can be very difficult. It is possible that the parent's life grinds to a halt, they become sad, depressed, lost and lonely without their children at home. They struggle to find their identity and to continue with the normal pattern of life. For them the crisis of a child leaving home can be crippling.

I do not want to sound morbid or depressing, I want to help you realise how important it is to choose wisely what you build your life on. There is nothing wrong with happiness, family or friends. In fact these are valuable and one should do everything possible to maintain these. But for them to be the sole foundation of your life, the fulcrum around which your life revolves, is very dangerous and almost sure to lead to sorrow.

It is for this reason that one needs to choose something that is of intrinsic value, is important in all situations and will never change. I wish I could tell you the answer, but it is something you need to discover for yourself. If you are told what you should base your life on, it would probably not be valuable to you and you are more likely to reject it. This is something that takes time to discover for yourself. You need to think clearly about it, weigh up all the options. For some people it will come very quickly, it will be blatantly obvious, for others it will take time, others will never find it. I recommend that at this point you put this book down for a day or two and come back to it once you think you have found the answer. If, in a few days, you are still unsure then don't worry. You can continue to read on, there are still a lot of things that we will cover which will help you achieve real, lasting success.

For now simply take some time to ponder the question: what is the most important thing in the universe that will never change?

Chapter 4: The Fulcrum Becomes a Guide

A Lost World

Today I sat with a young man who was very depressed and wanted to commit suicide. I had been asked by the local police to sit down and have a chat with him to see if there was anything I could do. I began by asking him some questions about himself. What I found out was very sad. He had come from a broken home. His father had left his family and run off with another woman, his mother was a drug addict who was involved in dealing drugs. His two younger siblings had been removed from their home and placed in foster care. His older siblings had been told to leave home. He himself had no schooling, no job and no future. Having been diagnosed with a learning disability he could not even read and write properly. He had no money, nowhere to go and no hope. The final straw was that his girlfriend, whom he had relied on for the last year and whom he loved dearly, had broken up with him, taking with her those he thought were his friends.

Here was a young man who was experiencing a crisis in his life. The problem was that this particular crisis was coming on the back of a life lived in crisis. As I spoke with the policemen afterward I said that this was a man without a fulcrum, a man with no long-term stability. We agreed to continue meeting over the next few weeks and months and I hope to help him find that one thing he can rely on in his life, the one thing that will help to balance out the back and forth of his life.

This young man epitomises the state of the world we live in. Many people are lost, they wonder aimlessly through life without a direction, without solid foundations for their lives. When the storms of life come along their world is washed away, broken and battered they move from one storm to another never finding firm, stable ground. It is my deep desire that everyone I meet finds the skills necessary to overcome adversity and to experience true, lasting success. This is my wish for you.

Some Temporary Solutions

By now I hope that you have spent some time thinking about the fulcrum of your life, the most important thing in the universe that will never change. If you have been able to answer this question for yourself I want to congratulate you, well done, you are on the right path. If, however, you have struggled to find that one thing, do not lose heart. It's perfectly normal for this important answer to take some time and in the meantime there are plenty of important things that can provide stability for your life while you search for that overarching goal.

If you have not found or discovered the answer to my question in the last chapter, might I suggest a few temporary answers that will do you well for the near future. Be careful, these should not be understood as being definitive. They too are inadequate for the long haul, for the 75 years on average we spend on earth. Firstly I suggest you don't build your life on money, sex, drugs, alcohol or any other form of instant gratification. While I wish it wasn't so, the best things in life take time, are hard work and are worth waiting for.

Secondly, I suggest that you build your life on close

relationships with people you know you can trust, people who are committed to being with you for the medium to long-term. While friends may be a powerful influence now, they often drift away, they find other friends, get married, have children and spend their time, money and energy on their own families. Family is a good foundation. While it is bound to change in the long-term, the change is usually slow. It can give a strong sense of purpose, satisfaction and contentment and is therefore valuable to real, lasting success.

The longest most stable relationships are usually, although of course not always, with your spouse. It is to this person that you promise to spend the rest of your life with, that you promise to be committed to until you die. This is a very good place to start when considering what to dedicate your life too. It is something that is very important and will only change over the very long-term (hopefully 50-60 years). The next best place to look is to your relationship with your parents. They have been with you from the day you were born and will probably be part of your life up until your late middle ages (50-60 years). They can be a source of great comfort and support and are an important part of anyone's life.

If you are not married or perhaps have no family, then do not lose hope. The general principle of relationships still holds true. Perhaps you cannot focus on a particular relationship, say with your parents or spouse, but you can still focus on relationships generally. Your friends, neighbours, and community are all valuable and worthy of your hard work. Perhaps you could volunteer in an area that supports relationships, a day care centre, a community hall, a local charity. In my opinion, helping others by coming alongside them, building relationships and supporting them is a good way to start. While it may not be a long-term solution, at least you will be doing something very satisfying on your way to achieving your personal goals. So, if you have not yet identified the universal principle of success in your life then I suggest you start here. You can use these foundations; family, spouses, general relationships to think through the principles I outline in this book. This way you will have something to implement immediately and can already start to direct yourself toward the ultimate goal of real, lasting success.

In order to have something to work with through the rest of this book, I am going to use a range of examples. Be careful, however, not to think that these examples answer the ultimate question: "what is the most important thing in the universe that will never change?" These examples are unlikely to answer our fundamental question. Rather, they merely demonstrate how the principles I outline can be applied in real practical situations. In some cases the examples may seem like the ultimate answer (friends, family, meaning etc.). In other cases I will use ridiculous answers to the fundamental question not only to demonstrate a practical application, but also to challenge you into remembering that success is not money, happiness, family, friends and relationships. Success is reaching your goal, even if your goal is, in the eyes of others, ridiculous.

The Measure of Success

Now that we have the fulcrum, the stabilising principle of life, it's time to learn to use it as a measure of success. This principle, which forms the core around which your life will revolve, needs to become the tool you use as a measure of how successful you are. This fulcrum needs to be at the forefront of your thinking, it needs to be on your mind every time you make a decision. It needs to drive your life, direct your thoughts and actions and become the fundamental purpose for your existence.

There are many ways in which you can do this and there are numerous resources and books out there that can help you. Some authors speak about a vision for your life, others about a mission statement. Some talk about guiding principles or fundamental values. Whatever way you put it, this needs to be the principle around which your life revolves. It needs to define your life. This is why it is so important that you choose wisely, it will guide every decision, drive every action and determine what success means for you. If you choose well, it will guide you for the rest of your life and lead you to good places. If you choose poorly, you will end-up with nothing to show for your life.

I do not want to prescribe a single method of utilizing this fulcrum. After all everyone is different. Some will prefer a vision statement, others a more general guideline, others will want to put down a detailed plan on how to proceed with their life. I do, however, want to give you some ideas as to how you can begin to shape your life around what is ultimately important and long lasting. Let's begin with an example of food as the fulcrum of our life. Let us say that you believe food to be the most important thing in the universe that will never change. You want to build your life around food, want to make it your goal, your ultimate goal, your measure of success.

What I suggest is that you start by clearly understanding the measure of success you have chosen. Clearly define it, quantify it, see it from every angle. What is it about that principle that you think is so important that it will never change for you. Ask yourself questions in order to better understand what it is about food that you love, why it is so important and why will it never change? For example, questions such as: what is good about food? What type of food is important to you? Why is it important? How much food is good? What exactly does it mean to be successful in food? How would we measure this success?

The answer to these questions may be as follows: I like healthy food, I love vegetables, home cooked meals, balanced diets, and the odd desert. It's very important to me because it helps my body to be healthy and means that I will be able to live a healthy, happy life. This in turn will allow me to live longer and enjoy healthy foods even more. It will never change because my body will always need food. While at some points in my life I may need different types of food, the basic principle of food is going to stay with me until I die. Because I am a man I should be taking in 2500 kcal a day, about 55g of protein, 75g of fat, 6g of salt and 33g of fibre. I think the best way I can be successful in food is to have a healthy, balanced diet on a regular basis. I would measure this against the recommended daily allowances and recommendations given to me by respected nutritionists.

Having taken some time to think about the basic underlying principle of life, that thing that is the most important thing in the universe that will never change, one is able to get a clear picture of what it means to be successful in this area. I now know that if I want to be successful I need to build my life around food, this means I need to eat, as often as possible, a healthy, balanced diet. To be successful means to eat well. This fundamental driving force can now influence every other aspect of my life. I can now choose a job that will allow me to do this (I need quite a bit of money to get the best food and at the same time need a bit of time to prepare and enjoy it) a good average job should be enough. I need to find a partner in life that loves food as much as I do, I need to find a house with a big kitchen rather than a big living room, and make friends with people who love to cook and eat healthy meals. I need to structure my leisure time around this, spend my free time cooking, reading cook books, watching the cooking channel, strolling through the supermarket and organic farmers markets. If food is the most important thing in the universe that will never change, and I live my life in the manner outlined above, I will be a successful person.

The same approach works for almost any ideal/goal you may have chosen. Let's say for argument that you feel your family is the most important thing in the universe that never changes. What family exactly do you mean? Is it mother, father, sister, brother, children or spouse? Why is it important? How do you know it never changes? What does it mean to be successful at family relationships? How will you measure it?

Your answers may be as follows: it is important because my family gives me a sense of contentment, supports me when I am in need, protects me, comforts me, builds me up and helps me to be the best person I can be. I know that it will never change because I have promised my wife that I will love and stay with her until the day I die. My parents will be with me for a very long time and my children will be with me when I pass away. To be successful at family means to cultivate loving, supportive, honest relationships with my family. This can be measured by the amount of quality time we spend together and how open and honest we are with each other.

In fact the approach / analysis even works with finances. Let's say you feel that money is the most important thing in the universe that never changes. You may ask yourself questions such as: Why is money important? How do you know it will not change? How much money do you need? What does it mean to be successful with money and how do you measure this success.

The answers you give may be as follows: money is important because it allows me to live the life I want to live. It allows me to buy the things I want, the food I need, the house I live in. Money will help me when I get sick by paying for my medicine. I know that money will never change because I will need it till the day I die. I need to earn more than the average person, I need to earn enough to take home about $50 000, $100 000, $1 million. To be successful at money means to make, or have, enough money in my bank so that I can buy the things I need and still have some left over for the things I want. To measure this I need to draw up a budget of what I need and then add a little extra for the things I want.

Now that you know more about your fulcrum you need to somehow keep it always on your mind. This means you need to remember it. You need to develop some way of making it easy to remember. So for example you may wish to write out a sentence, choose three or four words, draw a picture or even pick a single word. For example you may say that you want to dedicate your life to eating a healthy, balanced diet regularly. You may simply say that the three principles that are important for your life are healthy, balanced, and regular diet. You may simply use the words: healthy diet or perhaps create a picture which best illustrates this for you.

In our other examples you may say that you want to live your life in such a way as to cultivate loving, supportive and honest relationships with your family. You may choose the words: love, support and honesty in family, or simply good family relationships. You may choose a picture such as hands holding or people hugging to remind yourself what is important. The same is true in regard to money and finances. You may say that you want to live your life in such a way that you have enough money in the bank for the things you need and some for the things you want. You may use the words: enough, want and need, or simply the amount: $50 000. You could draw a picture of the pile of money you feel you should earn to achieve this.

It does not really matter which method you use; whether you create a vision, a mission or purpose statement, some guiding principles or an acronym. What is important is that you develop some system by which you can easily and quickly remember what you are living for. It should be so easy to remember and so ingrained in your thinking that were I to wake you up at two o'clock in the morning, shaking you awake and shouting "what is success" you would immediately, without stopping to think, tell me what success means to you. The principle of knowing, clarifying and remembering your defining principle, your fulcrum is half the battle. Simply by defining your goal you are much closer to true, lasting success than most people.

The next part of the battle, the second half of the key to becoming successful, is to make sure that this principle begins to define your life; let it guide your thinking and your choices. Spend your time, energy and resources on it and I assure you that you are much more likely to experience real, lasting success than if you simply tried to do everything you thought a good person should do.

So for example you should spend your money on food, give your time to finding healthy recipes, and put your energy into preparing balanced diets every day. If a friend asks you to go out with them to a party and it's dinner time, you should say: "no, I need to eat." If you only have money for a taxi or a healthy meal, spend it on the meal. If you feel like phoning your mother but it's time to prepare lunch, prepare lunch! If your wife and you are arguing but there is a good cooking show on television then watch the show. Eat a salad as she shouts at you, pop a few grapes as you stare at your overgrown garden. Whenever there is a conflict of interest, make a commitment to let this principle win out, don't allow it to be a choice at all, force yourself over and over again to put this principle first. If you must, and there is no other options, let your marriage fail, your house fall apart, your finances disintegrate as long as you eat a healthy balanced diet. You may have failed at your finances, your marriage, your family relationships, but at least you were successful in the most important area of your life.

It is for this reason that I cannot help but stress over and over again how important it is that you choose your fulcrum wisely; a poorly chosen fulcrum will ruin your life. Food is, unfortunately, a poorly chosen fulcrum. It is hardly of universal importance and will never really last throughout your life. In all likelihood you will end your days eating apple sauce from a straw. I use this example to illustrate the point, it is not meant to be taken literally.

Now, please don't miss-understand me. It is very rarely the case that you can only do one thing in your life. Usually there are a number of things you can do very well. For example, you will be able to have a good family, a great job, a nice house and still eat a healthy balanced diet. But make no mistake; you will not be able to do everything. If you want to succeed, you will have to give something up, you will have to fail at one or more areas in your life. Having a clear focus will help you make the right choice to ensure lasting, meaningful success.

It's no problem to build a hierarchy of important principles, say for example: food, family and money. But it is my experience that the more complicated the process the less effective. The more you need to remember and the more you have to think about choices in your life on a day-to-day basis, the more you fall back into old ways, just doing what needs to be done when it needs to be done. So keep it as simple and clear as possible and you are more likely to experience the success you are looking for.

Chapter 5: Know Thy Self

Not as Easy as it Sounds

In ancient Greece, there stood a mystical site called Delphi. It was a place to come and consult with the god Apollo. Etched into the walls were some of the wise words and prophecies given to those who came seeking advice. One of the most famous of these is the proverb: know thy self. Initially this proverb seems overtly simple. Surely everyone knows themselves? Why would this be such a profound proverb? However, on closer inspection the depth and importance of the proverb soon becomes apparent.

The one person you can count on to be with you until the day you die is yourself. There really is no one else on earth who you can guarantee will be with you on your dying day. Generally your parents die before you. Your siblings will move away, your children will grow up and leave home. One spouse usually dies before the other, and with a divorce rate of approximately 50% this leaves less than even odds that your spouse will be with you on the day you pass away. Depressing as it may sound, the truth still remains: most of us will die alone.

If you are going to spend the rest of your life with yourself then you had better get to know yourself. Getting to know ones' self, however, is not as easy as it may appear. You can't just have a conversation with yourself as you do with another person. You are not an object among other objects that can be described, investigated, and understood as you would a car, a boat or a house.

Furthermore, getting to know yourself is not simply a case of living with yourself. The more you live with yourself, the more you realise that you don't know yourself. The older you get the more you realise that you are not the person you thought you were when you were younger. When you were young you may have dreamed of taking over the world. Now that you are older you start to realise that this is probably a bad idea. When you were young you thought you could conquer worlds, save lives and change the face of the planet. The older you get the more you realise that you are not the person for that job.

It takes time to learn who you are and what your place is in the world. But this is time well spent. Knowing yourself is, in fact, conquering your world. After all, the world you live in is nothing more than the internal interpretations of external experiences. Although we share the same planet, your world is not my world because we are different people, we see things differently and as a result our worlds are different. To conquer the world we need to influence ourselves. Knowing who you are is one way to influence the world you live in.

The Three Components

Who you are as a person is a combination of three components, all of which you have very limited control over. Firstly, you are the product of your genes. For example you have a certain colour hair, height, and skin type. Genes play a role in a wide range of factors that make up who you are; from the big things (e.g. your intelligence) to the little things (e.g. what you like to eat). Did you know that very few people can taste cucumbers? To those who can't taste them, they seem mild, almost tasteless but to those who can taste these awful fruits, they are incredibly potent with a very strong taste. Some people can't handle red wine or milk, some people get hyperactive if they eat E-numbers. Some need more iron in their diet, some get down and depressed without potassium. All these things may be a result of your genetic makeup. While your genes play a key role in who you are, they do not determine everything. In fact the function of genes is to influence rather than control.

The second factor which influences who you are is your environment and experiences. Where you grew up, who your parents were, how many brothers and sisters you had and where you lived. Your school, your teachers and friends all shape the person you are today. Some positive, some negative. In most cases parents contribute positively to who their children become. In some cases these experiences have had a negative, even detrimental impact. Childhood trauma (e.g. bullying, an accident, having your heart broken by your first love) all leave lasting scars that may never heal fully. As a result you may struggle in certain circumstances, for example you may avoid close relationships, have low self-esteem, or perhaps you feel that no one will ever truly love you for who you are.

Your nature (genes) and nurture (environment and experiences) however, cannot account completely for who you are. Even identical twins, who have identical genes and very similar upbringings, are always two completely different people. There is something else that somehow mediates between your nature and nurture. A third, more fundamental characteristic, exerts a major influence on who you are, irrespective of your genes or your upbringing. Your genes and experiences may help to give you personality (black hair and a fear of heights) but this does not make you the person you are deep down inside. Personality and personhood are not the same thing. A cat has personality, a used car the same, but they are hardly persons. Call it your soul, your spirit, your inner being, whatever you will, but there is something unique in you that makes you the person you are.

We have little control over these three aspects of ourselves. Your genetics were given to you by your parents. Your upbringing and experiences are largely determined by others; teachers, friends, economic and socio-political factors. Your soul/spirit is hardly yours to command. It is simply there from the start. You may choose and control some things, that is true, but not everything. You can make changes to your environment; eat certain foods, dress a certain way, learn to behave appropriately. You can practice being polite, practice controlling your anger, learn to focus on important things and change some habits. However, you do not have unlimited choice and cannot control everything. For the most part you are who you are and you are just going to have to live with it.

This is not necessarily a bad thing. While it is true that your genetics may not have been the best in the world and you may have had the worst upbringing imaginable, you do not have a bad soul. I have yet to see a bad soul. I have worked with hundreds of people who have had genetic problems and difficult upbringings, but I have never come across a single person with a bad spirit. Although I have seen many people allow their spirit to be overruled by their genes or environments, I have yet to see a person who has been born innately bad.

There is, therefore, hope for everyone. Despite inadequate genetics or past experiences, your spirit can intervene and tip the scales in your favour. You are free to choose, to let your inner essence come to the fore, to make changes to your life and influence who you are and who you are going to become. What has happened to you in the past need not be the final word in your story.

Asking the Questions

In order to take control, or at least have an influence over your own life, you need to know who you are. This will allow you to make changes in areas of your life that you are not happy with, come to terms with past experiences and shape a brighter future. Really knowing yourself, however, is hardly easy.

Most people would have spent 12 years or more in school and a couple of years in further education, yet would never have learnt who they are, or even how to find out more about themselves. I am a governor at a local school and I can tell you that our schools are failing our children. There is very little personal development, very little time spent on helping our children get to know themselves and learn how to make correct choices in life. Schools may teach maths and science, even religion and philosophy, but they rarely teach the fundamentals of what it means to be a human being and how one can be the best human being possible.

There are numerous techniques by which we can know ourselves. The internet is filled with websites dedicated to the subject and questionnaires which you can fill out. There are television programmes, life coaches who can help, not to mention the vast number of books. Some of these are very good, but nothing can substitute the good old fashioned way: taking the time to think about it. Getting to know yourself is not something that will happen in a few hours or overnight. It takes time and effort, you have to spend time with yourself, you need to sit down and have a conversation with yourself (preferably a few conversations). You need to ask yourself some questions and question your answers.

I don't mean the basic questions such as "what's your favourite colour." I mean the really hard questions. For example: what do you think life is all about? Why do you think this? Can you change it? These, and a thousand questions like them, will help you to know who you are. For the purposes of this book let's look at some of the questions that are directly related to your ability to experience real, lasting success.

You need to understand what success is to you. If it's just about money, what would you really do with all the money in the world? I mean after the big house and fancy car? Fairy tales always end with "happily ever after," but this is not nearly as exciting as you may think. Can you imagine living day in and day out with nothing to do? Are you self-motivated enough to find something to do even if you don't have to do anything? Would you turn into a better person once you have all that money or would it become your curse? What happens to all your money when you die? What difference will it really make to you to have a larger tomb stone than everyone else? Is this really what success means to you?

Ask yourself honestly what success means. Is it happiness and if so what does that mean? Are you talking about life long contentment? If so, how will you achieve it and what will you do with it? Will you simply sit down and be content, or will you spread it, pass it on, teach others to be content? Does it matter how you get this contentment? There are prescription medicines that will do this, would this be the same as earning it? What kind of things do you think you need to do to get this contentment?

Here are some questions to ask about what success means to you:

- What is most important to you?

- Are you really the one choosing or have others made you think and choose this way?
- Is there a good and a bad way to live? Why do you think this?
- What do you want to do with your life and why?
- What will you do once you are successful?

I would encourage you to take a long time to think about what success really means to you personally. Try to understand why it is you think this way and if it is really a valid way of thinking. Does your idea of success really match up with who you are as a person? Someone with claustrophobia would make a terrible submarine captain. Someone who struggles with heights would be an awful pilot. So take a long to figure out what exactly success means to you and if it really matches up with who you are as a person. It is very important to know exactly what success means. The question: "What is the most important thing in the universe that never changes?" can help you know exactly what success means for you. Remember, that once you know what success is, you still have a long way to go in knowing how to achieve it.

Intrinsic and Extrinsic Work Patterns

Not only must you know what success is, you also need to know how you would go about achieving it. If you know yourself you will not only know what success really means to you, but you will also know how to practically achieve this success. By knowing yourself you will know how to get the most from yourself. You should know what works and does not work for you as you seek to achieve success. You need to learn about your strengths, your weaknesses, your key abilities and your failings. Knowing how to get the most from yourself is very important to understanding how you can achieve success. One way to know how best to achieve your idea of success comes from knowing your intrinsic work pattern as well as your extrinsic working style.

Your intrinsic work pattern is that aspect of your working style that is affected only by what is inside you, by your personality. While your extrinsic work style is how you respond to factors that are outside of yourself (your environment). Knowing yourself in great detail in these two respects can really help you to achieve success. It will empower you to make changes in your life (within yourself and in your environment) so that you can achieve greater things.

Here are some questions you can ask to find out more about your intrinsic style of working:

- Are you self-motivated?
- Do you find it easy to focus?
- Are you organised?
- Are you ambitious?
- Are you a morning, afternoon or evening person? When do you get the most done?
- Do you prefer to work under your own deadlines or someone else's and do you keep deadlines?

Once you understand your intrinsic working style, you can explore your extrinsic working style. Knowing what kind of environment you need in order to get the best out of yourself is vital. When you understand how you respond to your environment, you can make changes to your environment so that you can get the best results.

Ask yourself these questions:

- Do you prefer to work in indoors or outdoors?
- How do you prefer to work? At a desk, on the floor, on the sofa?
- Do you prefer music in the background or a quiet place to work?
- What kind of food helps you concentrate better?
- Do you prefer: pencil, pen, computer, tablet or whiteboard when you write?

These are just some of the things you need to know about yourself. If you find that you are a morning person and that you work best at a desk on a laptop while drinking fruit juice, then you can begin to make changes to your life so that this situation happens as often as possible. For example you may prepare yourself a glass of fruit juice before you go to bed at night, make sure you go to bed early and have a desk and laptop close to hand when you wake up. Then, when you wake up early in the morning, make sure you get straight to work, put off everything not important that can be done later in the day. Don't make your bed, clean the kitchen or even dress yourself (if you work at home-of course) just go straight to work. Work as long and as hard as you can and when your best hours have past, and you are finding it difficult to focus or concentrate, then go back and do the less important jobs at the time of day when you are not at your peak.

If you work in an office, then the same applies, grab your fruit juice as you rush out the door, leave your house in a mess and the newspaper unread, go straight to the office. Be as brief as you can with colleagues when you get in and go right to your desk. Start your work as soon as you can and stick with it for as long as you are able. Then, when your best hours are spent, go back outside and chat with your colleagues, have a good breakfast and spend the rest of the day on the unimportant things.

Personally I find that I am a night owl- I love to work at night. I also find it best to do my work while lying in a prone position, my laptop on my lap. I struggle to get up in the morning. So to get the best out of myself I begin my work at 11pm when the house is quiet and the phone has stopped ringing and I work for several hours. In fact, while I am writing this it is two o'clock in the morning. I work deep into the night until I am too tired to work anymore. Then I go straight to bed. I sleep late into the day. I will get up at about eleven o'clock in the morning (from half two to eleven is about eight and a half hours of sleep). I busy myself with mundane tasks for about an hour until I have fully woken up. Then when I am at my peak I begin to work. Since this is my best time and I am in a comfortable position that is just right for me, I will seldom take a break before four o'clock in the afternoon. Then, at that time I deal with unimportant things e.g. clean the house, water the plants, wash the dishes before cooking dinner for my wife who returns home from work at about five thirty. With my wife home I know that I will not get much work done; the television will be on, some friends may be coming over or we may go out. I don't try to get anything done during this time; safe in the knowledge that my best working hours are spent on my most important work. After my wife goes to bed the routine starts again. You may say that I am lucky enough to have a lifestyle that allows me to choose my peak hours, however, the reality is that I chose my career to make this possible because I knew myself.

I go to great lengths to make the most of my working style and as a result I get a lot done. Now be careful, I never said I get everything done, but the most important things are done and in general I experience a high level of success. Knowing myself is key to this process. It is a universal principle that does not only work for me but will also work for you and it will work in your situation. If you are able to learn about yourself, get to know what makes you tick, what success means for you and the best way of achieving it, you too will find it becomes easier to achieve what is most important to you. This principle works if you are a mother, a bank manager, or a CEO of a fortune 500 company and it works because it is tailored to you, the individual. It can only work, however, if you take the time to honestly get to know yourself.

Chapter 6: Take The Time To Think Things Through Thoroughly

Autopilot or Manual

Life has a funny way of forcing our hand. Whether it is at work, at home or on the playing field, life has a way of getting us to do things we never really set out to do. We are constantly bombarded with an increasing workload, more activities to do than we have the time to do, and pressure from all sides to get everything done. In the office we are constantly kept busy by emails, phone calls, fellow staff members and our boss. At home it is our partner, children and friends. Each day brings with it hundreds of individual activities, each demanding its own time, focus, priority and energy. From the routine of washing, sleeping, getting dressed, making dinner and paying the household bills, to the irregular duties of planning a holiday, watching the kid's football matches and the odd household breakage. The same is true for work, we have the regular duties (the monthly reports, the staff meetings, the daily administration) as well as the irregular activities; the new client quotations, the annual appraisals, and the daily emergencies that often seem like the end of the world.

The result of having to do so many activities every single day often leads to an autopilot approach. Do whatever comes next, in whatever order and for whosoever asks for it. Very few people are able to lift their head above the waves and see the horizon, where they are ultimately heading, to look to the future and decide on the best course of action. We simply do what comes along and we keep doing it until something else comes along.

In fact very few of us have even chosen the life we live today. For most people choice is simply a matter of doing what comes to hand, or at the very least, choosing between one or two alternatives. Take for example the way many people "choose" a career. Most will go to school and find that they are either good or bad at certain subjects. As a result of the marks they obtain they may choose to pursue these subjects into secondary school. Having achieved a certain score at secondary school, they will then consider which college or university course they would like to do, primarily in terms of what they are eligible do. Depending on which programme accepts them they will choose a university course and spend the next few years studying toward a qualification.

Those that go to university and those that do not, often take the same approach in choosing a job. They will look for their "ideal" job, searching the wanted adverts of their local newspaper or recruitment website. This may go on for a few weeks or months. However, eventually the need to find a job overpowers the desire to get one they like, and they become less picky about which job they will accept. They end up prepared to take any job that pays the bills and puts food on the table. They often take a job they don't like. Within a few years they have gained a bit of experience in this field, their salary has increased and they find they don't mind the work. When the time comes to find a new job they are faced with a tough dilemma: restart their career (often at a lower salary) or remain in their "chosen" field. Starting over is often a prospect which many find difficult. Over the years, as their income has increased, so too has their expenditure and a change of career almost always involves a decrease in salary.

As a result they seek employment in line with their current experience, experience gained in a job they didn't really want but had to take. As long as their job is not extremely awful and they can live with it, they prefer to maintain or improve their current salary rather than change jobs for a career that may be more fulfilling. The end result is a 40 year career in fridge manufacturing that ends with a mediocre retirement package and a gold plated watch. The rest of their lives are lived looking back over a long career which they never really chose.

Sadder even still is that this is not only the way most people end up in a career, but is also the way many people end up in marriage. Often people date only a few people in their lives. Eventually they find someone that does not break up with them and is not too awful, in fact they like being with that person. As the months turn into years, history begins to act as the driving force, forcing them to take the next step. It's easier to keep going on the path you are on than to change to a another one. In cliché terms: better the devil you know than the one you don't. The relationship follows a logical path which they follow as circumstances allow; first comes the engagement and the wedding, then comes a house and children. It's a logical progression and is easy to follow, it's not too bad, has some great moments and some awful moments, in short it is par for the course. They may tell stories of happily ever after with their partner, tell their family how lucky they are to have found "the one" but deep down inside they wonder if this is really what they chose.

In my line of work I frequently come across people who are

increasingly disillusioned with the life they are leading. On closer inspection it soon becomes apparent that they never chose their life. They made some choices, but really these were minor ones. Should they get married in a church or on the beach, should they buy a house or a flat, a dog or a cat? They never really thought about whether or not this is the best person to marry, or is this career really the best I can do with my life. They drifted into everyday life, doing what comes along, never really looking at the big picture, never asking how their life fits in with where they ultimately want to be. Since they fall into daily living, it is no wonder they fall into the big decisions as well; their career or marriage.

One day they wake up in a mid-life crisis. Their life is not what they wanted when they were younger, their family is not as they imagined it would be when they were teenagers. The future looks bleak, there is more time behind them than ahead and they start to question their life. Often they come to grips with this fact, resign themselves to the fact that their life will never be what they wanted it to be, they will not be the success they always hoped they would be. They settle back into their routine, let life take over and once more go with the flow.

Those that do decide to make a change often seek help. In some instances they come into my office or get hold of me some way. The good news is that there is always hope, you can always make a change, or develop what you have so that it becomes the success you always planned. However, it is better to do it sooner than later, to do it in your twenties than in your fifties, to do it now.

This change needs to start not only with the big things (the general direction of your life) but also with the little things. If you look back on your life you will see that it's the little things that got you to where you are now, the girl you met in the bar, the job advert you saw in the newspaper. It's the little things that seem to take over your life. The little choices lead to big ones and over time these little decisions become the general direction of your life. The key to influencing that general direction is to take the time to think things through thoroughly.

Think Before You Leap

These few words may well save your life. The basic principle is sound and the end result astounding. In every decision, the small, medium or large, take the time to think things through thoroughly today. Stop what you are doing and think, hold off on making that decision and think, wait for just a moment and…you guessed it: think. Thinking about what you are doing is fundamental to changing the general direction of life, to heading the right way, to overall success. As I have already mentioned, life has a way of forcing us into autopilot, forcing us to just go with the flow, to follow the daily grind. This is like an infectious disease. Once bitten, it takes over and it becomes difficult to do anything but follow the path set before you. The cure, however, is simple: take the time to think things through thoroughly today.

As I have said, this is not only fundamental for the big decisions in life- these decisions we often do spend a little time thinking through- but it is fundamental to the small, everyday occurrences that constitute our life. Just as I always encourage someone to think things through thoroughly before they take a job, buy a house, or marry someone, I encourage you to think things through thoroughly every time someone asks you to do something that at first appears small. When someone at work asks you to file a report for them, put something in the post, make a cup of coffee, speak to a client on their behalf, check over their work, write an email and make a phone call; it is imperative that you don't simply accept the task at face value, that you don't simply do whatever comes your way but that you really think it through.

You need to ask some key questions every time you do anything. Ask yourself: is this really important? Is it the best use of my time? Can someone else be doing this? Does it help me be more or less successful? Will this benefit me and my idea of success and how will it be beneficial? As soon as you start to do this, you will realise the amount of insignificant tasks you carry out that are of no true benefit to you at all. More than this; you will start to realise the true impact of the decisions you make and what led you to actually make them. As you use your guiding principle to decide what is important and what tasks you should do, what choices you should make, you start to grab hold of the general direction of your life. The end result is a direction aimed at lasting success.

For example, let's return to the example of food. We have said that the most important thing in the universe that never changes is food. We want to live to eat, we want to experience as much good food as possible and on our death bed we want it to be said that we ate well. Let's imagine that it is lunch time at the office and just before you go off to lunch a colleague comes to you and asks if you can join them to go shopping for clothes during the lunch break. Now, if you thought that people were the most important thing in the universe that never changes, you may well agree and join them on their shopping spree, forgoing any sustenance you may want. However, because you know that food is your guiding principle, the most important thing in your life, you know that the correct answer is a great big resounding "NO!" food comes before friends.

You may think to yourself, well we can do both and it is true that often both can be done. However, sometimes a clear choice must be made. If food is important and if your life's ambition is to eat well; a hamburger on the run is just not going to cut it. You need a steak for lunch, you need to sit down, to eat well, to enjoy it as much as you can. This way you know that you have achieved your life's goals today, you have done the most with your day, lived the best life you can. You may have failed at being a good friend but you have succeeded in eating well and that, according to our example, is far more important.

If, however, you feel that friendship is far more important than food and you have made this your life's goal and ambition, then the choice is easy. Grab a snack, eat it in the taxi and spend your lunch break with your friend. You may have failed to eat well but you have succeeded in building your friendship.

Whatever the decision, the answer is to take the time to think things through thoroughly today.

Chapter 7: Five Principles to Help You Think Things Through

I believe that there are five principles that can help guide you as you take the time to think things through thoroughly. Remembering these principles can help you make the right choice, they can guide you as you follow your life's ambition. I have found these principles key to making decisions, and especially when it comes to weighing up what is and is not most important. The underlying premise is that we should always keep the most important principle first. Try to remember these principles as you think about the choices you make.

The First Principle: Never Trade the Future for the Present

There is nothing wrong with enjoying what you have at the moment and living a good life, but it is important that you do not risk the future for the present. We all know that things come along that require attention. These may be work related (such as a deadline) or they may be personal (such as a fantastic opportunity to go on holiday or spend a bit of time in another country). Life is to be enjoyed and lived. Therefore you should grab hold of these opportunities and sometimes simply focus on the here and now. However, whatever you do, do not trade your future for these present opportunities.

Whenever an opportunity appears that requires your attention, you should stop to consider the true implications. For example, if your boss asks you to work on a Saturday but you have set Saturday aside as your barbeque day, or perhaps your family day, you need to ask yourself if this is a once off responsibility that will allow you to ultimately reach your goal, or if this may set a precedent that will ultimately hinder your success.

In my job I work on Friday and Sunday nights. My wife is a teacher and works Monday to Friday. This means that the only day we can have together is a Saturday. So that we can have one day a week together, I do not work on Saturdays. However, in my line of work there is always something happening on a Saturday, someone to visit, a conference to attend, a function to organise. Usually I am very clear about my Saturdays and don't mind failing a few people and letting a few others down so that I may spend time with my wife. After all, she is one of the most important things in my life.

However, a few weeks ago an opportunity came up for me to go to London on a Saturday to attend a conference. It just happened to be the same Saturday as my wife's birthday. Of course there was a decision to be made. This conference would be a good opportunity for me to work on a broader goal in my life but it might also affect an important aspect of my life; the relationship with my wife. Luckily for me, in my marriage, dates are not important. My wife and I have no real sentimental value associated with birthdays, anniversaries and holidays. We don't mind celebrating these at different times. After talking to my wife I decided to go to the conference and I made sure that the next Saturday would be an extra special day for us. However, it is important that I remind myself that Saturday work is a very rare occasion. Even if my wife does not mind me doing it, it simply cannot become a regular event. My wife, according to my life's ambition, is far more important than my work. I can take one or two opportunities to work on a Saturday but if it becomes a regular occurrence I may well be choosing my present over my future. I will be choosing to work on Saturdays over the long-term future of my marriage.

The key is not to make hard and fast rules. Don't force yourself to always choose one thing over another or to give up the opportunities that come along. The key is to think about life as it happens and to look at the decisions we make carefully. Spending one Saturday, even if it is the Saturday of my wife's birthday, would not risk my relationship with my wife (our marriage is much stronger than a missed birthday). However, if I begin to make a habit of this, begin to miss every other Saturday and then move on to every Saturday, very soon there will be no days left to spend with my wife and my marriage will definitely suffer. If this were the case I would be trading my future for my present.

Of course, I have taken these decisions because I feel my marriage is important. However, one may say, and I am not sure why they would, that their career is more important than their marriage, or perhaps, and this is the game we are playing together, food is more important than their marriage. In which case it would be completely in line with their life's goals and ambitions to ignore their wife every Saturday and spend the entire day cooking, eating or attending conferences. Personally I feel this would be a poorly lived life, but I am not here to make judgements on the lifestyles of others. I am simply trying to help one to achieve their own personal, lasting success, whatever that success may be. Taking the time to think things through thoroughly is an important part of that success.

The Second Principle: Two Lowers Never Trump a Higher

It is good to have a hierarchy of what is important. One may for example say that family, career, community and fun are one's top priorities- in that order. This gives us a few areas to concentrate on instead of being too narrowly focused. It also allows us to achieve more in a wide range of goals. However, there are some drawbacks with having a hierarchy.

Some people work on what can only be explained as a "points based" hierarchy system. They may, for example, believe that food is 10/10 on the scale of importance and that work is an 8/10 and friends 6/10. This kind of thinking can lead to a false sense of success. Let us say, for example, one is required to choose only two of these three. For example one may have to choose to leave work at the normal time, go home and spend the rest of the evening cooking and eating or they may choose to work longer and then to go out with friends to a club, forcing them to grab some fast food on the way to their friends. The logical choice for many is to be successful at two things rather than one. Therefore they may choose the latter option, work longer, spend time with their friends and eat junk food. However, if you take the time to think things through thoroughly, you soon realise that this is not a good choice. If they choose this option they achieved success at work (8/10) and friends (6/10) giving them a total score of 14/20. In percentage terms they are 70% successful. If, however, they leave work and go home to eat, they would have experienced success in the most important part of their life, giving them a score of 10/10, a 100% success rate.

Of course, this is may not reflect reality, it may be only playing with the maths and not necessarily reflective of real life. Let's turn it around. Let's say they believed that family was the most important thing in the world, that friends were second and work was third. This is, surprisingly a common hierarchy which I see often. Often these three principles are in conflict and we can only be fully successful at one, reasonably successful at two or partially successful at three. A large number of people prefer partial success to full success. They try to do it all, work late, meet friends, get home in time to kiss the kids good night. Sounds like a good plan, they did a full day's work, met their friends and still showed their children that they loved them. By our societies standards such a person would be a resounding success, a good person.

However, if we think it through properly we soon realise that in reality they are far from a resounding success. They have only been partially successful at each of these three things. They may have been very successful at completing their work commitments, reasonably successful at building their friendships but would have only done the bare minimum when it comes to the family. If family was really at the top of their hierarchy of success, then bare minimum is just not going to cut it. Over the course of their life they will realise that it is not possible to be successful at everything. They will inevitably fail at the most important thing because they were too afraid to fail at lesser things. They will end up spending more time with their friends and less time with their family, more time at work and less time with their children. Work will begin to squeeze their family life and friendships will seem more important than an evening at home with the wife and kids.

If you must make a choice, then take the time to think things through thoroughly and always choose the most important thing. Anything and everything else is simply bonus. Being 100% successful at the most important thing is far better than being 60% successful at everything. On the one hand you are a 100% success, on the other hand you are only mediocre. So remember this principle, two lowers do not trump a higher.

The Third Principle: Compromise with the Least Disadvantage to Your Key Purpose

This is a world of compromise. There is simply no way of getting around it. We are continually asked to compromise. Whether it is at work, home, or recreation we cannot get everything we want. We need to compromise. This in itself is not a bad thing. Compromise presents us with different opportunities and helps us to find a reasonable path through life. However, if we compromise in the wrong places (which is often the case) then we may find that our long-term success is negatively impacted. Not compromising is dangerous but compromising in the wrong place is even more so.

If you must compromise (and only if you must), always do so with the least disadvantage to your key purpose. Let us say for example that, a person feels that the most important thing in the universe that will never change is food. The second most important thing is TV and the third is sleep. Let's say that such a person comes home from work at about eight o'clock at night. In order to get at least 10 hours sleep (which they consider to be optimal) they need to be in bed by ten o'clock so that they can wake up at eight o'clock in the morning. In order to cook and eat their favourite dish they need at least two hours. They soon realise that they cannot cook and eat their favourite dish, watch two hours of TV and sleep ten hours. A choice must be made. The logical choice would be to cook a different meal (taking at the most one and a half hours) then to spend one and a half hour hours watching TV and sleep for 9 hours. This would be acceptable where getting some of everything done is the best approach.

However, according to this person's hierarchy of importance, the most important thing they can do with their life is eat well. Sacrificing this so that they can achieve secondary goals means that they did not eat as well as they could have and as a result they were not as successful as they may have been. In this case the best answer is to cook their favourite dish, watch two hours of TV and sleeping only eight hours. If they do this, they would have been fully successful in the most important area of their life, done a good job at second and an acceptable job at third. The result would have been a very successful person who has achieved all they could for the most important thing in their life and on top of that, achieved some success in other areas.

This simple illustration can easily translate into a practical situation. Let us say Dad gets home at seven o'clock at night. He is tired and hungry but his children go to bed at eight o'clock. If he believes that his children are the most important thing in his life, far more important than his personal well-being, then he is better off holding back on his meal and relaxation and spending the hour with his children until they go to bed. If his body cannot cope, then he might take a snack while spending time with his children (such as a sandwich in one hand as he cuddles the baby in the other). By doing this he has achieved all he can for his family. He would have compromised his own personal well-being, having to carry on a little longer while tired and hungry, but he would have a strong, healthy family and, since this is most important to him, it would mean he is a resounding success.

Situations like these are very common place in today's society; situations where we have to choose between different important options. Children, personal well-being, financial and work responsibilities often conflict and we need to compromise somewhere. The key to being successful is to take the time to think things through thoroughly and choose a way forward which has the least impact on your most important goal. If some compromise must be made, try as hard as you can to compromise in everything except your most important goal. Do whatever you can to be as successful as possible in the most important thing first. Everything else is a bonus.

The Fourth Principle: Importance Trumps Urgent Every Time

We have all had those days, you know what I am talking about, the days where you were so busy your feet never stopped to touch the ground. Every time you thought you had it under control another emergency popped up. You spent the whole day running around doing things that must be done. Then when you finally came home and thought back over the day, you could not remember what you had done. You felt as if you had been busy all day but accomplished nothing. The things you set out to accomplish were left undone; the really important tasks of the day still await you tomorrow. The reason is clear: you spent the day on crisis management rather than problem solving. The whole day was spent on one crisis after another, each more urgent than the last, but ultimately not important to the bigger picture. These are common days, days we all experience, all the time, and days that need to stop. If you live your days like this, you'll live your weeks like this and eventually your years.

Firstly let me let you in on a little secret of life: there will always be another crisis, another problem, another emergency. You can bank on it! At some point in the next 48 hours someone is going to come running to you to solve their urgent problem. It's just a fact of life. Now, here is another secret (and this is the big one); you can't solve all these problems nor do you need to. You can, in fact you should, fail. Failing at non-important urgent problems is one of the best things you can do to reach long-term lasting success. Looking at the big picture, taking an active stand on where to fail and where to succeed, is the best way to ensure long-term success. Getting bogged down in the daily trenches of crisis after crisis is the best way to ensure a life poorly spent.

So the next time someone comes to you with a crisis, something you absolutely have to solve right now, or you find yourself struggling with an emergency, you need to stop what you are doing and take the time to think things through thoroughly. Ask yourself this question: is this important or is it simply urgent? If you did not solve this crisis what is the worst that could happen and how does this compare to failing at the most important thing in your life?

Principle Five: Important Trumps Enjoyment Every Time

Let me end this chapter on an unpopular but necessary note. Something I often need to remind myself: importance trumps enjoyment every time. In the world we live in we are continually tempted to have as much fun as we can. There is more on the TV than we can possibly watch, more magazines than we could ever read, more chocolate and ice-cream than we can eat in a life time and more games to play than can be played. We are continually tempted to sit back, relax and enjoy ourselves. I remember walking through a mall a few weeks ago and I was suddenly struck by how often the word "treat" appeared in the shop windows. The ice-cream parlour called to me to treat myself, the local café encouraged me to have something special, even hair products urged me to do something different because I am worth it. The message was clear, sit back and relax, spend your money on something special in every shop.

The thing about special is that it's only special if it's special. Special goes with the words: irregular and every now and then. A few months ago my wife and I took a trip through Europe. We stopped in Belgium and bought some chocolate, then we moved on to visit some friends in Switzerland and of course we bought some chocolate there. After Switzerland we went to my brother in Germany and added to our stash. By the time we got home we have more than seven kilograms, over fifteen and a half pounds, of the finest chocolate in the world. For the next six months, every time we went to our local grocery store, I would see "normal" non-special chocolate on sale. We did not purchase this "normal" chocolate because we had all that fine European chocolate at home. After six months of eating the best chocolate in the world I was looking forward to finishing our stash and eating some regular chocolate again. Then, when I visited my parents in Ireland, my mother gave me a big bag of Swiss chocolate as a gift. Of course, I could not refuse it, doing so would be rude and ungrateful, and after all it was Swiss chocolate, but it was not nearly as special as it could have been had I not spent the previous six months gorging on such good chocolate.

The point is this: something is only special if you don't have it too often. The same is true for enjoyment. The proliferation of advertising in our world encourages us to enjoy ourselves all the time, to take time off, to get away, to relax and forget about what's important. In fact, often they claim that these things are what's important. Remember that these are advertisements; they are not really looking out for your best interests. If you always put aside what is important to enjoy what is not, you will find that eventually you will have neither enjoyment nor achievement.

Now, this is not to say that you cannot enjoy yourself. Of course you can. You can take some time every day to relax, this is important. A relaxed body and a refreshed mind will work better and achieve more. Indeed, I hope that you find achieving in life's most important things very enjoyable- I certainly do. This, once again, highlights the importance of picking the right answer to the all-important question I posed at the beginning of this book. Finding that thing in the universe that is most important and that will never change will give you great joy in your life.

However, just as over indulgence in chocolate will make you fat and cause you to lose your appreciation for fine sweets, too much of the wrong kind of enjoyment is not good for you. This kind of enjoyment and relaxation is meant to be a temporary thing, an opportunity for you to recharge your batteries so that you may continue along the road to achieving your gaols. It's not, in itself, the goal of life. So if you find that the most important things in life are being left undone while you are enjoying yourself, then it is time to take charge, to take the time to think things through thoroughly and choose what is important over what is fun.

These principles cannot be underestimated. If you want to experience real, meaningful and lasting success, then remember to keep the important things in mind as you face everyday life, as you are forced to make compromises and choices. Often it only takes a few extra seconds to think about what you are doing, a minute at most. So take one minute to save your life's dream, to achieve all you need to achieve and take the time to think things through thoroughly today.

Chapter 8: The Problem with No

No to Every Yes

One of the major factors in the success or failure of someone is not in their ability to manage themselves, although this too is a major contributor, but rather their ability to manage their environment. No one lives in a perfect situation, we all have things that get in our way when working toward our goals and hinder our ability to be successful. There are numerous factors which hinder our ability to be successful but the most complex of these is, without a doubt, the human being.

We live in a social world made up of other people and these people have an immeasurable influence on us. Our friends, family and work colleagues all have an impact on us; urging us to give up some of our time and energy for them and their needs. We interact with them on a daily basis and have to constantly mediate between their needs and ours. They require us to do things for them, to run errands and engage in tasks which they can't do themselves. In many cases they require our help and are, in some sense, reliant on us. Some of these activities are things we like to do, for example spend time with our friends. Other activities we do simply because we want to help, for example help a colleague with work. All of these activities require our time, energy and resources and as such take time, energy and resources away from other activities, activities that may be potentially more important.

If we could properly manage this important aspect of our environment, if we could take control over what activities we do for and with other people, we would be free to spend this time and these resources on activities that are vital to our success.

There are two possible extremes, both of which need to be avoided. One extreme is the person who never helps others. This person says a resounding "no" to every request of their time and energy that does not directly benefit them. This person can be considered selfish and self-centred, serving only themselves. Very soon they will find themselves isolated and alone and can hardly be considered to be successful in any true and proper sense of the term. Ultimately their humanity begins to wither, for the human being is- at the heart of his/her being- a relational being. Without serving others we cease to serve ourselves (our true self). When we have no true, healthy interpersonal relationships, we become impersonal and our personhood fades away.

At the other extreme is the person who always helps others. The person who never gives a healthy "no" to the demands others place on them. Their time is taken up completely by others, their resources are spent on other people. Such a person ceases to be an individual and becomes the salve of their community, the network of relationships they inhabit. Their life ceases to be their own and becomes a life lived through the lives of others. As they constantly choose between their own need for self-actualisation, self-fulfilment, and the needs (often petty needs) of others around them, they cease to experience true success (the self-actualisation that comes from achieving one's goals). They fail to understand that community is made up of individuals. It is true that these individuals must serve each other or there is no community, but they must retain their individuality, live their own reality and meet their own needs; in short they must be their own person.

They cannot live solely and wholly for the community. Such a reality is like being a drop in the ocean, the drop disappears altogether and only the ocean remains.

For us to experience real success there must be some healthy mediation between the needs of those around us and our own needs. We need to say "no" to some of the demands of others and "yes" to some of our needs. It is important, however, that this balance is understood clearly.

The True Meaning of Balance

Many people think that when someone speaks of balance they speak of a 50/50. In other words they believe that when I say that there needs to be a balance between the community's needs and our own, we should be saying "no" to the community 50% of the time and "no" to ourselves 50% of the time. While on the face of it, this logic may seem sound, in reality it is neither possible no appropriate. A dying mother who is in the last few days or months of her life will need a lot of attention and it is only proper and healthy that, in this circumstance, we give our time, energy and resources. Saying "no" 50% of the time in this situation will be detrimental to this mother and is simply not appropriate.

A simple mathematical equation cannot solve this problem- as maths often fails to solve the problems of life. People are not machines and they cannot be treated as such. We need a more robust approach to balance between needs of those around us and our own. An approach not based on numbers and figures but on guiding principles. We need to look to our fulcrum, our guiding principle, to help us choose when it is appropriate to say "no" and when we need to say "yes," both for the needs of others and for our own needs.

In many cases the guiding principle someone has chosen (that principle which is the most important thing in the universe that never changes) will, on some level, be based on other people. It is almost impossible to find a truly valid guiding principle that does not, in some way, include the needs of others. We are community people, relationships are at the very heart of what it means to be human and to be successful people. No matter what we choose as our own personal success, it will in some way be impacted by, and have an impact on, other people.

While the needs of a dying mother, in almost all circumstances, must demand our time and resources, the needs of a lazy work colleague do not. There are hundreds of situations where people approach us for help and require us to give of our time, energy and resources to actives that are not important to our life's goals. These situations require us to give a resounding "no." In my work as a business consultant I am always astounded at the many situations work colleagues are faced with that pressurise them to say "yes" to another colleague, to spend their time, energy and resources on an activity that is of absolutely no benefit to themselves. A number of examples come to mind. I think, for example, of colleagues who ask for help before they go away on holiday, or colleagues who require assistance with the most mundane tasks such as working the coffee machine in the canteen, or setting up their email accounts. Colleagues who seek assistance to find paperwork which they have lost, or with office equipment that is broken (the printer/photocopier is particularly prominent in this regard). These are regular issues that come up in my discussions with businesses men and women around the world.

This is hardly limited to the office. I think of parents roped into numerous PTA meetings and committees to discuss issues that are so dismally unimportant that it makes one's head hurt. I personally have been involved in PTA meetings which were spending large amounts of energy and resources on fundraising for a school with a budget of 5 million that is not in financial difficulties. At first glance this may seem like a noble cause, but on closer inspection the futility of raising a few thousand become apparent. 15 parents, 20 hours of meetings per parent, and 4 events hardly merits the time spent. This is particularly pertinent when one considers that the parents were feeling under pressure, did not have the time and felt that their contribution was not valued by the school. My advice for this group was simple: back to the drawing board. Find out what exactly you want to do, find out what the best, most valuable use of your time and energy is and do that. If it is fundraising then so be it, but if it is creating a space for parents and teachers to meet, then fundraising may in fact be stealing your focus and energy and you need to say "no." PTA's, community projects, and local charities are all valuable. We need them for our community to be strong. Yet this does not mean that we need to give a disproportionate amount of our time and energy to groups and organisations that are not central to our guiding principle. Of course, if they are central to your guiding principle, say for example you want to live your life serving your local community (a noble and valid cause) then I would certainly encourage you to give every last minute you have to these organisations. However, if your goals are different, say for example you wish to have a strong and healthy family, or perhaps you wish to write an award winning book, then perhaps limit the time you spend away from your family or writing table.

Work and community are only two places where our time and energy is demanded. Our family and our friends too require a lot of our time and energy. It is much easier in these situations to be coaxed into always saying "yes." After all, we love our family and friends deeply, we want to help and want to support them.

Yet many demands are made on our time that are of no value to the ultimate goal of having good, valuable and healthy relationships with our friends and family. Friends are particularly bad at this. Often they will ask for our help in an activity which they can do themselves (paint the house for example) or call on us at a particularly inconvenient time. Often these requests come at the expense of our family, for example asking us to help them move a sofa on a Saturday. You may think; well I had no plans, the family was simply staying at home, so why not. The fact of the matter is that when it comes to family, plans do not build good relationships, time does. Spending time with each other around the house and just being in each other's presence is just as important as going on a trip or watching your son's football match. Helping your friend move their sofa may not be as important as sitting around the house doing nothing together with your family.

Of course I am not saying that one should not help their friends or family. Doing this is very important and is key to good relationships. However, if for example, your life's ambition is to write a book and yet you have so many friends that all your free time is taken up helping them paint and move sofas, something has to give. Either you give up writing your book and fail at your life's ambition or you need to learn to say "no" to your friends at some point.

There is simply no getting away from it. We cannot do everything. We need to make choices, we need to choose between different demands on our time. This inevitably means having to say "no" to someone. This may be a work colleague, a community group, a friend or a member of our family. If we want to achieve something worthwhile, if we want to be individuals who experience real, lasting success we will need to say "no" to something. We need to let some people down and fail at some things so that we can succeed at others. There is simply no alternative, failure is not an option because it is ultimately an inevitability at some point, in some area of our lives. The key to true success is to choose where we fail and where we succeed. To choose where we say yes and where we say no.

Even though we realise, and logically accept, that one has to say "no" in some circumstances, the actual act of saying "no" remains difficult. We are often faced with a situation where we don't want to do something and understand clearly that we should say "no", yet for some reason (often beyond our comprehension) we still say "yes." What is it about the word "no" that we find difficult to say even when we know we should?

Fearing No

There are a number of reasons why saying "no" is difficult and in order to overcome this and express our "no" properly, we need to understand these reasons. So let's spend some time looking into these reasons. Let's begin with the first reason; the fear of rejection. Human beings, as I have said before, are community beings. We are beings which require relationships. Relationships are so central to our existence that isolation and loneliness is fundamentally damaging to our psychology. One need only look at the world we live in to understand that this is accurate. The reason social networking sites have become so popular so quickly is because they offer a way for human beings to make connections. People who feel isolated and alone, for whatever reason, may go online to make and meet new "friends" quickly. Social networking sites are popular because they offer us a quick solution to a fundamental human need, the need for other people to love and accept us.

Inherent in the need to be involved in community, even if this community is a virtual community such as is the case in social networking sites, is the need to be accepted by this community. We need others to accept us, to like us and to consider us to be valuable members of the community. We need to be liked. In fact some of these sites even have a button one can push that allows us to "like" something our friend has done. This fundamental principle is prevalent throughout our society and indeed throughout the world. Being liked and accepted is so important that, in my opinion, it is a fundamental driving force behind the billions of dollars spent in the advertising industry every year. Advertisements focus on the needs of the customer to feel liked. Much of the underlying psychology behind an advertisement is that if you buy this product, or use this service, you will be liked, you will be accepted. Wear this dress and you will look great, as a result people will like you. Buy this deodorant and girls will like you. These shoes will make you a winner, everyone likes a winner.

Since we want to be liked, we are afraid of people rejecting us. When someone says "no" to us we often take it as them rejecting us. For example, if I ask a girl for her telephone number and she says "no" it means that she does not like me, that she rejects me. Feeling rejected is very hurtful and causes a great deal of mental and psychological anguish. It's not easy to overcome this rejection and it is for this reason that men find it difficult to approach a girl they like and ask her out. Just as I don't like being rejected, I don't like rejecting others. If someone asks me something, I am inclined to say "yes" because I feel that if I say "no" to them I am rejecting them, and if I reject them, they may not like me anymore.

When a friend or work colleague asks me if I can help them, I am afraid that if I say "no" they will no longer like me. This is because I think about how I respond when a friend or work colleague politely says "no" to my request. I realise that I am inclined to dislike them for it. I feel rejected, disliked and hurt. I seem to think less of them for it, seem to feel that they are not as great as I thought they were, not as nice, valuable and good as I had assumed. Since we tend to dislike people who say "no" to us, we don't want them to dislike us for saying "no" to their requests. As a result, we often are afraid that if we say "no" to someone they won't like us for it.

The fear of being disliked often prevents us from saying "no." However, it does not always follow that saying "no" to someone will lead to them disliking you. While we may tend to dislike those who say "no" to us, this is not always the case. For example our parents have said "no" to us on countless occasions and (in most instances) we still like our parents. Just as we don't always dislike everyone who says "no" to us, others don't always dislike us just because we say "no" to them. If we are able to understand this clearly we can free ourselves of the fear of being disliked when we say "no." We can begin to understand that saying "no" does not necessarily mean losing our friends. In fact I believe that the manner in which we say "no" is far more important than the mere fact of saying "no"- I will get to that shortly.

Empathy and Sympathy

Another key reason why we struggle to say "no" is that we have empathy rather than sympathy for our friends. It is not easy to explain the difference between sympathy and empathy, indeed many people have their own understanding of these terms. However, I do believe that it is helpful to have some distinction. My understanding of the two concepts is as follows: empathy is when we feel what others feel. It is a strongly emotional connection between what someone else is experiencing and what we are feeling. For example, when my friend tells me that they have lost their job, I empathise with them if I feel upset and saddened. I feel the sense of worry they feel, the sense of loss and rejection and as a result I want to help them to alleviate these negative feelings. Their problems become my problems, their struggle my struggle.

However, if I sympathise with them I do not physically feel their emotions. I can see how such a situation is difficult, how it could create feelings of worry, loss and rejection but I do not personally experience these feelings. Their situation remains their own situation, their struggles remain their own experience. I am inclined to help my friend because I can understand what they are feeling, but their feelings are not my feelings.

A distinction between these two principles is important when saying "no." On the one hand, if I have empathy with my friend, my reason and decision to say "no" will be based on emotion, emotions that I personally am experiencing and feeling. I will feel emotionally involved in the situation my friend is facing and as such will be much more inclined to spend a large, and perhaps disproportionate, amount of my time, energy and resources on their situation. However, if I have sympathy with my friend's situation I can understand what they are going through but I do not feel what they feel, I do not carry their burden for them. I am far more logical in my approach to whether or not I spend my time, energy and resources on their situation.

Now we should be careful here. There are times for empathy and times for sympathy. If a friend is faced with a serious situation, such as the loss of a job, a breakdown in family relationships, a death in the family, empathy is both appropriate and healthy. It is good to cry with your friend when they are in serious trouble, to spend your time and energy helping them in their hour of need. However, this does not mean that empathy is necessary in every situation. A work colleague who is struggling to find the paperwork she lost may not need your empathy. A Neighbour who would like to write down your chocolate cake recipe right now because he has a visitor tomorrow does not need empathy.

Empathy is simply not appropriate in all situations. In fact, there are very few situations in which empathy should replace sympathy and these are almost always very serious situations. In most situations we face in life, in the day-to-day living, sympathy is best. Understanding that the problems our community faces, in most cases, are not serious and that they are not necessarily our responsibility. We do not have to cry with every person, do not have to take responsibility for every single request that comes our way. We are individuals, we have our own problems, our own concerns and in the normal movement of life, much of what is asked of us is not that important.

If we empathise with every situation, make every situation our own, we will become subject to, and slaves of, these situations. We will no longer be able to cope with our burdens because we will be carrying the burdens of others, and most seriously, the unimportant burdens of others. We will not be able to achieve the success we want to achieve, to reach our own goals, because we will be too busy trying to help others with their unimportant, yet urgent, problems. We are not responsible for everyone else's problems and we are certainly not responsible for the unimportant problems others face. We must say "no" to these unimportant burdens if we are to achieve any true success.

The Taboo of No

In terms of some of the reasons why saying "no" is difficult, I wish to say one last short and final word. In many cultures, certainly in the western world, the word "no" is culturally a difficult word to say. There is, in our cultures, a sense that this word is taboo, a word that should never, or at least very rarely, be said. A few years ago my nephew, who was then only two years old, got into the habit of saying "no" to everything. The reason may be that it was one of his first words, or perhaps it was the only word he knew that gave him power over the world around him. If someone wanted to hug him, he would say "no," if they wanted to play with him; "no", watch television with him; "no." No matter what the activity, his response seemed to always be "no." Of course, to the adults around him this response was very frustrating as we wanted to respect his wishes but at the same time wanted to spend time with him and to take care of him. Very soon, within only a few days, it became apparent that this could not continue and soon he began to get in trouble for saying "no." His mother, and those who were looking after him, began to re-educate him about the usage of this term. To them he could say "no" only in the most basic of situations. He could say "no" to more ice-cream (although of course he never did), he could say "no" to seconds at dinner, to wearing a blue shirt rather than a green one or to the type of book we were reading with him. Beyond these simple situations he was not allowed to say "no." Whatever adults wanted him to do he had no choice. If we wanted him to bath he could not say "no," to go to sleep, eat vegetables, play with an aunt or uncle the word "no" was not allowed. A "yes" was the only answer. After all, we thought, adults are in charge and other people are more important than ourselves (and in this case himself). After speaking to a few parents about this, I realised that this situation is quite common. Most toddlers learn to say "no" then proceed to use it incessantly, needing a similar correction to the one given to my nephew.

While I understand why we need to make sure that a toddler learns to listen and obey those around him, after all his very survival depends on it, I am not sure that the principle learnt at such an early age is one that should stick with us. Teaching children that "no" is inappropriate leads to adults who believe that "no" is inappropriate and results in a society that cannot say "no." Of course my task here is not to correct an entire society, or even to encourage us to always use the word "no." Rather I am simply trying to help us to see why it is that we struggle with this word and why it is that we need to use it appropriately

Yes and No Go together

If we are to use "no" appropriately we will need to understand something very important; as this chapter heading suggests, "yes" and "no" go together. These two terms are intimately connected. It is impossible to say one without the other and every time you say the one, you are in fact saying the other as well. "Yes" and "no" are paired twins. Like identical twins are two different people and yet closely connected, "yes" and "no" cannot be separated.

Let me explain. If my two year old nephew comes to me before dinner and asks to have a chocolate, I will of course have to say "no" because it will ruin his appetite, and in the long run he will learn to eat chocolate instead of a healthy diet- this will cause serious problems. So when I say "no" to him I am in fact saying "yes" to his health. The same is true when he asks me to stay up later than his bedtime, while I say "no" to extending his bedtime, I say "yes" to his general wellbeing. If I say "no" to the sweets, fizzy drinks, salty snacks and fast foods, I am in fact saying "yes" to him, I am saying "yes" to his being healthy, "yes" to his future, "yes" to loving him.

This same principle is true when adults say "no" to each other. Saying "no" automatically means saying "yes" to something. If I say "no" to helping my neighbour paint his house I am in fact saying "yes" to something else. This may be a "yes" to spending time with my children, to cleaning my house, to working on an important project, to volunteering in the community, to writing my books, or to spending time with myself. Of course, it may also mean a "yes" to something far less important, such as watching the latest episode of Star Trek or the newest reality TV show. It may mean, and this would be unfortunate, saying "yes" to being lazy.

When my friend asks me for help I need to understand clearly what I am saying "yes" to and what I am saying "no" to. If I say "yes" to my friend, what am I saying "no" to? Could it be that I am saying "yes" to helping my friend pick out a pair of shoes, but "no" to my exercise routine? Or I am saying "yes" to spending time with my friend at the local bar watching the game and "no" to spending important time with my family. What are the consequences of saying "yes" and are these more or less important than the consequence of saying the "no" I inevitably say.

Knowing When

It is very important that we say both "yes" and "no" appropriately. It is important that we answer our friends, work colleagues and neighbours with both "yes" and "no," but how do we do this appropriately, how do we tell when it is time to say "yes" and when it is time to say "no." The answer, of course, is touched on at the beginning of this book. We use our guiding principle to judge every situation; from the small favour to the big, from the little things to the gigantic. We use it as our compass, as our means of measuring between what is important and what is more important.

Remember, it is impossible to get everything done. One simply cannot do everything that is required of them in life and in the same way we cannot answer "yes" to every request made of us, even the requests we would very much like to oblige. The bottom line is that we are going to have to let some people down some time, we are going to have to fail at some things so that we can achieve at even more important things. Let's look at the following example to illustrate what steps need to be followed when someone asks us for a favour.

Let us say that it is dinner time and just before you begin to prepare for yourself your favourite meal the doorbell rings. It's your best friend and he is standing outside in the rain. His car has just broken down and he needs a lift to the cinema immediately or he will miss the cheap deal for the movie he has been dying to see. What do you do? There are two options. Firstly, you can leave your dinner, take your friend to the cinema, join in with the movie and eat popcorn for supper. Secondly, you can say "no" to your friend and close the door on him, leaving him in the rain with no lift to the cinema.

Of course most of us would grab our car keys, and head out the door. Drop the dinner and make sure that our best friend catches his movie. However, if you have made food your guiding principle; you believe that the best life you can live is one that is dedicated to eating the best food possible, and as much of it as possible, leaving your dinner may not be the wisest decision. Doing so would surely be a "yes" to friendship but it would be a resounding "no" to food, to your life's goals, to your ultimate ambition. If you said "no" to this ambition once or twice there may be very little impact, but if you started a habit of saying "no," of skipping lunch breaks in the office to work, of missing dinner to spend time with your friends, or breakfast to sleep longer, pretty soon your life's ambition will dry up and you would have missed numerous opportunities to eat the best food. If food really is your most important principle then it may be that you have to say "no" to your friend.

Whenever you are asked to do something you should never reply immediately. You should take the time to think things through thoroughly and respond with a "yes" to the most important principle in your life. It may only take five seconds to think about it, but it will help to ensure lasting, real success. Ask yourself the basic question: if I say "yes" to this, what am I saying "no" to? Choose to say "yes" to the most important things and "no" to the things that are unimportant. Any other course of action, over the long run, will negatively impact your ability to succeed. "Yes" and "no" are opposite sides of the same coin; we simply can't say one without the other. While it is often easy to say "yes," it is very difficult to say "no." With this in mind I want to help you to learn to say "yes" to failing in unimportant areas by saying "no" to unimportant requests.

Chapter 9: How to Say No!

"No" is such an ugly word! It has connotations of rejection, dislike and is culturally despised. It's the kind of word that most people struggle to even say. Not only is it a word that we don't like saying but it's also a word that we don't like hearing. When someone says "no" to us it's as if they don't like us, as if they are rejecting us. As such it causes us to respond in accordance with these feelings. Since we don't like to say it, and we certainly don't like to hear it, most of us avoid the word altogether. However, if we are to be successful in life we need to say "no" to the unimportant requests that continually come our way. The challenge to us is to say "no" in such a way that the person who hears it does not take offence. In my research on this topic I have found that the best approach to this difficult topic is given by Leland and Bailey in *Customer Service for Dummies.* Let us explore a modified version of their approach which includes four key steps to saying "no."

Step 1: Empathy

The first thing to remember is to show empathy. When we say "no" to someone it will have an effect on them. It may be that they are worried, struggling or desperate. Our "no" may make these feelings worse. For example, let's say your work colleague wants you to help them find a document they lost. This document was never in your possession and it really has nothing to do with you. More than this, you are working on an important project that demands your time and if you said "yes" to your friend, you would in effect be saying "no" to this important project. Saying "no" to the project you are working on may lead to severe consequences to the client, the company and perhaps your job. You simply must say "no" to your work colleague. Even if they are your friend, what you are working on is more important and demands your full attention.

Your colleague is probably worried, they may feel that they are responsible for this document, that the boss will get angry if they can't find it and that ultimately they are going to get in trouble. Having someone help them look for the document increases the chances that they will find it and that they will get out of trouble. As a result it reduces their worry and would make them feel a whole lot better. When you say "no," their fear and worry will remain- the chances of finding the document diminishes and the chances that they are going to get in trouble increases. In short they will be negatively impacted by your "no." It is very important that you let your work colleague know that you understand the situation, that you know they are worried, that it is an important document and that their situation is both real and important to you. You have to show them that you understand how they are feeling.

Therefore, before we say "no," we should always start by showing that we have some understanding of the situation, or at least the feelings others are experiencing. Begin with an empathetic statement. Say something like "I know that you are worried about finding this important document..." or perhaps "I know that this document is important and that you want to find it quickly..." A sentence along these lines goes a long way to helping the person realise that you do care, that you do understand and that you are not just being unkind when you say "no."

Step 2: Reason

While the human being is not a machine and does not work on reason alone, reasons do have an impact on our ability to understand others. When we have information about another's situation we are far more likely to empathise with them and as a result accept their answer. Reasons demonstrate that our response is not arbitrary, that we have thought about the problem and that we are not randomly choosing to say "no." When we give others a reason for what we are saying we add weight to our statements and help others to accept them. However, this only works if we include a reason that is viable, logical and makes sense. This means that when we say "no" to someone, we should demonstrate that we are in fact saying "yes" to something far more important. Our reasoning should be simple: I can't help you because I have something more important to do.

This latter point is very important. If the activity we are doing, and the reason we are saying "no," is not more important than their request, they will undoubtedly feel undervalued and believe that we are being selfish in our thinking, or worse that we simply don't like them, that even though we know their request is important, we don't think they are important and therefore we are simply going to say "no." Demonstrating to them that we have a valid reason, that we are busy with something more important is vital to helping them understand why it is we are saying "no." This means that we need to use this word "important" in our answer to them. We need to clearly say that we understand their situation but that we are working on something "very important" and that we can't stop working on it, as the consequences will be very severe. You may for example say something like this to your work colleague: "I am working on an important project that must be finished by Friday, if it's not done properly the company could lose a lot of money…"

Step 3: Fairness

The third thing to include is some sort of demonstration of your being fair. If someone says "no" to us, we often wonder if it's because they don't like us personally. Perhaps they understand our situation, perhaps they have a reason but even still it may be because there is something wrong with us. We may, as a result, take it personally. Most of us don't want people to take our "no" personally. We want them to understand that we are simply working on something very important and if we don't attend to our task the consequences might be quite severe for us. In order for them to understand this, it is important that they know we are being fair, that we are not just saying "no" to them but that we have and are saying "no" to other people in similar situations. This means that you need to tell them clearly that you have told other people the same thing as you are telling them. You need to say something to the effect of "I have also had to say no to John…" or perhaps "John has just asked me to help him on a marketing campaign but unfortunately I had to say no to him…" Another way of saying it would be to say: "because this is so important, I really can't help anyone for the next few days…" Something along these lines will go a long way to helping your colleague understand that you really do have to say "no" and that it's not because you don't like them.

Step 4: Restoring Control

Finally, and most importantly, you need to somehow restore control to the person. The word "no" seems so final, so forceful. Hearing it is like hearing that we have no more options, no choice in the matter. When we make a request and the request is turned down there is a sense that we don't have control over the situation, that the world is telling us what to do, that we are simply pawns in a great, big game where we have no say in what happens. After all, someone else has decided our fate, someone else has rejected us, someone else has prevented us from moving forward. This feeling is difficult to cope with as it goes against our need to have some control over our life. As individuals we need to have some control of our circumstances and do not take well to situations where we feel controlled by others or events. Being unable to control our circumstances can cause great anxiety and stress which makes us less effective.

When we say "no" to someone we need to give them an option, we need to give them a way to manage their feelings, another route to take than simply being frustrated with us. We need to restore their control and give them a sense that something can be done about the situation. We could suggest that they ask someone else, or perhaps to ask them to come back later, or even that you may be able to help in another way. For example, you could say: "can you ask Paul to help?" or perhaps "is there any way you can come back on Wednesday when I may be able to give you a hand?" Another way to put it would be to say "I can't help you look for the document but I can ask Sandra, my assistant, if she knows where it is." Any statement that, in some way, gives the person back some control, or offers some light at the end of the tunnel, will go a long way to helping them accept your "no."

Putting it all Together

Let's put it all together using the example given above. Your colleague comes to you to ask if you can help find a document they are missing. However, you are working on an important project that demands your full attention. Your "no" could be worded as follows: "I understand that this is an important document and that you are eager to find it. However I am working on the Thompson account which is due on Friday and is an important project for our company. It is taking up all my time and energy, so much so, that I even had to turn Paul down who offered to take me out to lunch. Perhaps Steve could help you out or I could ask Sandra if she knows where it is or if she knows someone who may be able to help you."

Here are some other examples:

"I know that you and Bill haven't had a night out since the baby was born and that it's important for you to relax every now and then. I would love to look after little Sarah, however, I have had a really busy week and next week looks even worse. I need to recover or it will affect my health, I even had to turn Joanna down who asked me to come over and bake with her. Do you think you could get a professional baby sitter for tonight, or perhaps move your night off to next week when I can take the baby?"

"Mom, I know that you hate that sofa and that for the last five years you have been looking to get rid of it, but I have not spent enough time with James this week and I promised to take him to the zoo, I really don't want to let him down. Dad asked me to go with him to the game this week but I had to turn him down. Do you think you could get a neighbour to help you move the sofa, or perhaps pay a removal company, I could contribute to the expense if you would like?"

These responses may sound long winded, and indeed a

simple "no" would have been much quicker. However, putting it this way helps to ease the effect, will preserve relationships and avoid the negative impact that may be associated with our "no." Ultimately, however, there is no getting around it. We need to say "no" if we are to be successful at the important things in our lives, we need to fail in some areas so that we can succeed in others. While you can take a few seconds to think about your responses before giving an answer, my advice is to say "no" as soon as you know it is necessary. Don't put it off too long. Its best to say "no" as soon as you know it's what must be said.

Chapter 10: Some Practical Tips

In this chapter we will look at some practical steps that you can take to increase your chances of achieving real lasting success. I have selected what I think are the most important top principles that lead to either true success or failure. I believe, and I have seen evidence, that if you are able to grasp hold of these principles, you are far more likely to succeed. These are basic principles that may be well known to us but, for whatever reason, we often fail to remember or implement them. So take the time to think them through, consider the practical implication of each principle and ask yourself this question: "what would my life be like if I could put this in place every day?"

Say No...to Yourself!

In the last chapter we looked at the immense importance the word "no" has on our ability to succeed. I simply cannot overstate how important it is that we say "no" to the unimportant requests others make on our time, energy and resources. By saying "yes" to everyone and everything we will ultimately fail at what is really important. Success and failure go together in much the same way as "yes" and "no" go together. If we want to succeed we have to fail and therefore we have to say "no" to something.

On the one hand we have to say "no" to the unimportant requests of others, but on the other hand we have to say "no" to the same requests we make of ourselves. This, however, is often far more difficult than saying "no" to our friends, neighbours and colleagues. I believe that the reason it is so difficult to say "no" to ourselves is three fold. Firstly, we are unaware of making requests of ourselves. Secondly, our environment promotes self-gratification and lastly, we tend to be more sympathetic to ourselves. Let us look at each of these points in more detail.

Firstly, we are often unaware that we are making requests of ourselves. It's easy to see and hear the requests of other people because they come to us externally, often in some formal manner. For example, the doorbell will ring and a person we know will be standing before us with a request, or a colleague could knock on our office door, or perhaps the phone rings and a member of our family speaks to us about something they would like to ask us. Since we don't see these people standing in front of us every minute of the day, we are alerted to the fact that this is an abnormal occurrence, we therefore have to pay attention.

However, it's been a long time since I knocked at my own front door, called my own phone or spoke to myself face-to-face. Rather, I simply know what I want to do and, far more importantly, I don't even ask myself if I can or should do it; I simply go ahead and do it. So for example, I will notice that the oven needs to be cleaned, or the grass needs to be cut, a chair needs to be repaired or, far more likely, my favourite TV programme is about to start. I don't necessarily ask myself whether or not it's a good idea to do these things, I simply do them.

Secondly, as we previously discussed, we live in a society that promotes instant self-gratification. What the ancients called hedonism, the desire to enjoy life by having as much fun as possible, we have turned into a viable and valuable lifestyle, which is deeply ingrained in our culture. Everything around us screams out: enjoy yourself now! This idea is so ingrained in our culture that we often don't even know it. For example we say things like "as long as you are happy" in answer to an ambiguous or even taboo situation. This answer is given to our children who want to quit their music lessons because they are too hard, to a couple divorcing, or a friend who is dating two people at the same time. We very rarely say "that's wrong" (unless it is blatantly so, as in the case of murder, rape etc.). I have come to realise that whenever someone says to me "as long as you are happy" it more than likely means they do not agree with the choice I have made.

Far more than simply making ourselves happy, we have to make ourselves happy now. "Just do it" and "why wait" are the foundation of capitalism. We are continually urged to spend our money on what makes us happy and spend it now. This is undoubtedly part of the problem with economic recessions. The Credit Crunch was caused by people who were encouraged to buy a large house, or flat screen TV and encouraged to do it even if they could not afford it. After all, if you can't afford it now, just take it on credit and pay it off later. Whatever you do, do it and do it now.

This spending philosophy leads to us doing the things that make us happiest now and putting off the things that need to be done for later. I prefer to do the gardening now than study that new course I wanted to study which would lead to me getting a better job later. Learning a new language is not fun, and although I really want to learn it in the long run, right now I would prefer to fix the table, go out with my friends or simply listen to music. When choices are presented to us between that which makes us happy now and that that which makes us happy in the long-run, our culture encourages us to choose the here and now.

The third reason we don't easily say "no" to ourselves is that we are far more likely to be sympathetic to ourselves than others. Since we live in a society that promotes individualism and instant gratification, we far more selfish than we should be. The requests of my friends, neighbours and colleagues are not nearly as important to me as my own requests. I am emotionally far more engaged with myself than with others and as a result I can hardly have sympathy with what I am experiencing but continually have empathy. It is not a case that I simply understand my desires (as may be the case with others) but because I am personally experiencing them I cannot help but empathise with myself.

This means that I am, both by nature (physically experiencing the desire to do whatever I want) and by nurture (the culture encouraging me to satisfy my own desires) more likely to give in to my desires. In simple terms: I do what I want to do. If my friend asks me to help them change the carpets in their new house, I may in fact want to say "no" even though I feel the obligation of friendship making it very difficult to say "no." However, if I asked myself to fix the oven light that has been bothering me for months, I don't want to say "no" at all. It will be a distraction and besides more enticing than sitting down to work.

All this means that a lot of my time, energy and resources are spent not only on the requests of others, but on my own unimportant requests; what I want to do, what I ask myself to do, and what I often do without formally asking. When two options are presented to me; to learn a new language, or go out with friends; to search the "wanted" pages of the local newspaper for the 50th time or watch TV, I am more inclined to pick the easier, more enjoyable option every time. This option, however, is often the least important and as a result I find that I choose to succeed in the least important aspects of my life and as a consequence I fail in the most important.

If we are going to succeed, really succeed at what is important, we have to choose to fail at what is not. We will have to choose, often, to fail at taking the easy road and having the most immediate fun. We have to choose to fail at fun and succeed at lasting contentment. We have to choose to fail at enjoying ourselves for now and succeed at achieving our long-term goals. Simply put, we have to say "no" to ourselves and say "no" often. We have to fight both our nature and our nurture and fight the urge to enjoy ourselves for now, not only every day but every hour of every day. We need to deny the instant gratification that we so often crave and force ourselves to bellow out a resounding "yes" to our true, long-term, important desires. Your general success over the course of your 80 odd years on earth is determined by your "yes" and "no."

Of course it's not necessary that we always say "no" to the enjoyable things in life. By saying "yes" to some fun we may be saying "no" to stress and therefore "yes" to good health. This is indirectly saying "yes" to better success. However, in many instances a "no" is not only important but also the right thing.

I have found that there are a number of practical things we can do that will help us achieve this. Firstly, never do anything (and I mean anything) without thinking about it. Don't brush your teeth, eat that chocolate, watch that TV show, open the mail, cut the grass, cook the dinner, chose which dress to wear, or make a cup of tea without thinking about it. Stop for half a second and ask yourself if this is the best thing you can be doing with your time and energy. In many cases the answer may be a "yes." Brushing your teeth, eating a good dinner and getting dressed are all activities that are often important. However, in many cases the answer may be a "no." It is better to have an uncut lawn and the weeds over grown in your garden than to miss your son's football match. It is better to miss every episode of your favourite TV programme than to never learn the language you so very much wanted to learn. Better to have a healthy body by spending so much more time eating well and exercising than to have read every one of the Harry Potter books. These books may be well written, they may give you great joy, but if you spent your time eating properly and exercising you will live longer and enjoy the benefits of a healthy lifestyle. Always think about what you are doing before doing it.

Secondly, as with saying "no" to others, you need to ask yourself what exactly you are saying "yes" to and what you are saying "no" to. As with the example giving just above, if you say "yes" to recreational reading what are you saying "no" to? Is it that you are saying "no" to family, to friends, to learning a new skill, to achieving some greater goal? Are you saying "no" to something far more important than what you are saying "yes" to? Understanding the true consequences of your "yes" will help you to make better choices and accomplish far more. Be clear about the real implications of what you are doing and you will be far more likely to spend your time on activities that are fundamentally valuable and of intrinsic benefit to your life's ambition.

Thirdly, and perhaps much more importantly, grow up. One of the tough things about being an adult is that you have to do things you don't want to do. Part of the maturing process is the ability to fight against your emotions and to make the right choices, to do the things you may not want to do but you know you have to do. We often don't want to go to work in the morning, don't want to deal with the traffic, the paper work, the boss who does not appreciate us, the client who is demanding beyond reason. We deal with taxes, pensions, mortgages and our personal finances. We act as good parents to our children and loving partners to our spouses even when we don't want to. We iron our shirts, clean the bathroom and make our own beds. A large portion of our days are filled with activities we don't really want to do but have to do. This is simply the consequence of growing up and taking responsibility for our lives.

In the same way when you think about the activities you choose to do and the true consequences of the "yes" and "no" choices you make every minute of your day, you soon realise that if you want to be successful you are going to need to do a whole host of things you are not going to like. I don't mean unethical things, I mean hard things. You are going to need to give up a lot of free time, a lot of fun activities, some time that you spend with your friends, some time watching TV and time reading good books. If you want to be successful, if you want to achieve your life's goals, no matter what that might mean, you need to say "no" to the you of today, to what you want to do now, and say "yes" to the you of tomorrow, to what you have to do. Saying "no" to yourself is simply a part of this process, it's simply something you have to do. So remember to get over it, to do what must be done, and say "no" to the hundreds of unimportant requests you make of yourself every day. Remember to grow up and do what you have to do, even if you don't like it.

Murphy Lurks Everywhere

I hate Murphy. He has haunted me my whole life. Everywhere I turn, every plan I make, no matter how important, Murphy has a way of messing it up. I may plan a barbeque on Saturday and even though the weather report says it will be sunny, Murphy will ensure it rains, or the barbeque will break (contrary to how unlikely that may seem it has happened before).

This guy seems to rule the world, seems to be playing havoc with all our lives. Murphy's law, this unwritten rule, states that "if something can go wrong, it will go wrong." You may not know his name, may never have heard of Murphy's Law, but your life has, at some point, been affected by it. Whatever can go wrong will go wrong. Since Murphy lurks everywhere and his name has become well known, it's important that we factor it in to our plans.

Plans are great, in fact they are vital. Without good planning one is bound to fail. I believe, along with many others, that a lack of planning is the number one reason for failure. Now I am not talking about the good kind of failure, the kind where we plan to fail or consciously take the decision to fail. I am talking about total, disastrous failure. One of the reasons I have spent so much time in this book on the guiding principle of your life, the most important thing in the universe that will never change and the fact that you should think things through thoroughly, is because planning is so important. Knowing where you are going is half the process of planning and half the battle for lasting success.

But, no matter how good your plans are, you should not be fooled into thinking they are fool proof. Murphy lurks everywhere, and if he can, he will ruin your plans. You should never be fooled into thinking that achieving lasting success and reaching your goals is as easy as it sounds. Something is probably going to go wrong- I can almost guarantee it and if your plans do not take this into account then whatever goes wrong may be detrimental. If your plan is riged and inflexible and you believe that there is no possible chance that something can disrupt it, when something does disrupt it (and believe me it will) you will be devastated and may find it nearly impossible to get back on track.

We need to take the time to think things through thoroughly and this means looking at our plans with a critical eye. Not only should you be asking yourself if what you are doing right now is the best you can do with your time, energy and resources, but you should also be asking yourself: "what can go wrong?" Having asked this question, we can begin to take steps to prevent it from going wrong.

It's not really necessary to worry about what can go wrong with the smaller day-to-day things (although these are the things that usually take up a lot of our time and in this way negatively impact our life's direction). It's not important to ask yourself what can go wrong with brushing your hair, or putting on your shoes or even making your breakfast. If something goes wrong (for example your shoe lace snaps) I trust you are mature enough to see it for what it is: not a big deal. These small troubles only really become important if we let them.

It's the big things we should be wary of; the important decisions we make, the key goals we have, the serious plans we put in place. For example you may think that you will be in your current job for three years and then look for a new one. You may say that it's only to raise a bit of money so that you can start your own company, or take that world trip you wanted, or buy that new house. In a plan like this, spread over three years, something is going to go wrong. You may fall pregnant, you may become sick, you may suddenly get a tax bill, inflation may go up, the price of the house you want might rise, you may be presented with an opportunity you can't refuse, the country's economy may fall etc., the list is endless. You simply cannot assume that the position you are in will only last three years, or will last at least three years, both assumptions are likely to be proved wrong. Things never go the way we plan, and what we hope for is often far from what we get.

In the game of life anticipation is your best weapon against Murphy. Let me give you a simple example: I often have to pick up more than one thing from my desk and carry it to another part of the office. For example, I often have to pick up my laptop, its power cable, a stack of paper and, of course, my coffee mug. When this precarious situation presents itself to me my mind rushes to my good old friend Murphy. Chances are I am going to trip over the cable, bump into someone, my hands are going to get tired quickly and I am going to drop something. In situations like these I always remind myself of what I can drop and what I can't drop. I take a split second to think things through thoroughly, and I tell myself that I can drop the paper, the laptop cable and even the mug but I cannot drop the laptop, that's just too important. If I feel the mug begin to slip, or the papers begin to fall, I never risk the laptop to save them. If the mug drops it means 5 minutes of cleaning up and a broken mug is easily replaceable. If the laptop drops it may mean serious expense and hours of work to get it back up and running normally. Drop everything, I say, but keep the laptop safe.

This is a simple example that has thousands of applications in the regular day-to-day running of our lives. I don't put a glass on the edge of a table, don't hold a soft drink can with two fingers, I never remove my favourite pen from my desk (it will only get lost) always put my keys back where they belong, always take a second to look at what I am throwing away, set two alarm clocks when I have an important meeting in the morning, never let the car petrol tank fall below a safe level (in case the nearest station is shut), always put a little bit of money aside for emergencies etc. There are literally thousands and thousands of small things I do in my daily life as I go along to minimise the impact of my old friend

Murphy.

Not only do I think about these little things, but I also think about the big things, the general direction of my life. I have a plan and a vision for what I want to do with the one life I have. I am clear about the most important thing in the universe that will never change and I try, as hard as I can, to ensure that I am successful in this area. This means that I have to lookout for Murphy and whatever might go wrong. My wife could fall pregnant, my house could burn down and destroy both my computer and my backups- decades of work could be lost. Any one of these, or a whole host of other possibilities, could happen and have an impact on my life's goal and direction.

With this in mind, while I am enjoying today, I am always thinking about the future. I have spent a lot of time looking at what the most important thing in the universe is that will never change, and I have chosen something that does not depend on my financial status, where I live or what job I do. My house could burn down and I could lose all my important documents, but I would still be able to achieve my life's work. Others, however, may not have chosen this type of goal.

Perhaps you have built your life on a single career or a specific job. If this is the case ask yourself; what would you do if you became ill and could not work? What will happen to your life's ambition when the economy collapses, when your country goes to war, when your bank goes bankrupt, when your pension plan is embezzled, when you retire? Note that I have not formulated these questions as an "if" but a "when." It is inevitable that something is going to go wrong; you simply cannot avoid this. What plans do you have for these eventualities?

To have the best chances of achieving lasting success one needs to be prepared for when things go wrong. This means spending a little time, energy and effort in trying to make contingency plans. For the little troubles in life small contingency plans are sufficient. Make sure you have a little more time in your diary for meetings that start or finish late. Make sure you have a little extra cash in your pocket in case you can't get to an ATM. Keep good backups of your files and put aside a little bit of money every month for things like emergency dentistry, a broken washing machine, a new computer etc.

For the big things in life you need bigger contingency plans. If you lose your job try to make sure you have some savings, or some assets to get you by. Try to educate yourself beyond what you do now so that you have something to fall back on if something goes wrong. Try to have a life insurance plan in case you fall ill, or medical insurance for you or your partner in case you need it. Don't place all your life's investments in one pot, and most importantly, try to choose a life goal that is not dependent on money, finances or your health.

It's good to have hobbies and interests that reach for the stars. For example, I have always been interested in studying further. Some people run marathons, climb mountains or cycle the tour de France. I like to study. A new book is my next mountain, the PhD my Olympic games. However, studying is not my life's ambitions. My life is more than a competition, a certificate or a new book. Choose goals for yourself that are really worthwhile and flexible. That way when Murphy comes knocking he will not knock you down.

Watch Out for Lost Days

Finally, remember that failure is not only a part of life but a good part of life that you need to choose. Some days you are going to lose the battle with Murphy, some days will be completely lost to your life's goals and ambitions. Emergencies will happen, things will go wrong and you will go off course for a little while. This is not the end of the world. Accept these days for what they are, understand that everybody has them and there is nothing you can do about it. They are what they are, and we all need to take these days- these failures- in our stride. Some days you may feel too down to get out of bed. On days like these, my advice is to live these days with the least disruption possible to your mental health. If you really are too down to get out of bed call in sick, take a personal day and spend the day sleeping. As long as it does not cost you too much, simply write it off. As every company loses clients, every country goes through recession, every person experiences days which are wasted.

The important thing is to remember that you have had these days in the past and you will have these days again. This means that you need to make up for this lost time in some way. The best way to do that is to put more energy, effort and resources in on the days that are productive. When you find you are on a roll (the day, month, or year is going well), you need to do everything you can to ensure these are the most successful times of your life. You need to ride the wave of these days for as long as you can.

Let me give you a simple example. The key to writing a book is to write often, if possible every day. However, there are many days that it is impossible to write. Meetings, events, emergencies, family etc. all take up your time and you find that it's possible for days to go by that you can't write. One of the hardest things to cope with when writing a book is feelings. Some days you just don't feel like writing and on these days finding words can be very difficult. Sometimes you may sit at your computer for hours and only come up with a couple of sentences if you are lucky. These are often lost days. However, there are days when the writing flows easily, when you are able to write as fast as you think. On days like this you need to spend as much time as you can writing. Leave the dishes unwashed, don't answer the door, forget your email, cancel the unimportant meetings, forget the post and banking, just sit and write for as long as you can. If you ride that wave of inspiration, you do enough work to overcome the lost days and in the end it balances out and you achieve your goal of writing that book.

So don't take failure too hard, don't beat yourself up because you have had a bad day and did not get anything done. Write it off, watch TV and eat some ice-cream. Tomorrow is another day and if you work hard on the good days and have more good days then bad, you can easily afford a few bad days without seriously risking your long-term success.

Chapter 11: Avoiding the Traps

While we may need to write off some days, it's important that we don't write off days unnecessarily. Some days, weeks or months, we can fall into a trap that forces us to spend our time, energy and resources unnecessarily. I am not talking about important things wasting our time, things like our family needing our support, or even a once in a lifetime opportunity that presents itself. I am talking about the traps of everyday life, the common areas we all struggle with, areas that, if unchecked, will take up our time, force us to focus on unimportant things and ultimately lead to lasting long-term failure. These traps are so common that every single one of us struggles with them, most of us never realising the true impact. If we are to avoid writing off days or weeks unnecessarily we need to be conscious of the top ways in which our time, energy and resources are wasted. We need to defend ourselves against these unnecessary traps and be continuously vigilant to ensure that we do not fall prey to them unwittingly.

Trap No. 1: Socialising

The first of these traps is by far the most common and most serious: socialising. We are all social creatures and as a result we all want to spend as much time as we can with other people; connecting, sharing and socialising. As creatures of community it is important for us to socialise. It validates us, sets our place in the community, makes us feel wanted, special and valued and strengthens the ties we have with each other. In short it is vital for our mental health and our survival and therefore no one should be without someone else; be that friend, family or partner. This aspect of our lives is so important that it demands our time and is therefore both the great joy of our life but also the greatest danger.

A large portion of our time spent socialising is good but a large portion of this time is both unnecessary and unimportant. Socialising, as we have all experienced can get out of hand and before we know it our lives are negatively impacted. Rather than being built up by the time we spent with others, when we let it get out of hand, we are torn down, feel drained and have no time for anything else. This is particularly true in the modern age of electronic communication. With SMS and text messages, email, social networking sites and other social media, we often spend our time on the mobile phone or computer to see if anyone has contacted us and "poking" them when they haven't. Social networking sites, for example, are so large that almost one seventh of the world's population use them and in the United States, so a recent survey showed, the equivalent of 100 000 years were spent each month on the largest site alone. Just imagine what could be done with that kind of time and energy?

Our obsession with communication and socialising is not always healthy. Spending hours on social media is just one obvious example. However, the distraction of the mobile phone in our pocket, constantly on and constantly beeping, has a detrimental effect on our ability to focus on the tasks and activities we need to do. Writing a book for example is particularly hard if the phone keeps ringing, so is learning a new language, painting a picture or the daily routine of work and life. The phone ringing its annoying tunes distracts us from our family, from our job and even from our shopping. I cannot tell you how many times I have been in a grocery store wondering around, lost in my own world, texting and SMSing my friends. I always laugh when I realise how stupid I must look and cry when I get home and realise that I forgot the most important thing I was meant to pick up. This same principle is true for email. We constantly check our email, constantly push the "refresh" button on our mail server when we all know we should be concentrating on something else. In fact, while writing this very paragraph, without realising that I was logged into my Skype account, a phone call came through from my father and we spent a protracted amount of time talking about unimportant things.

The obsession with socialising is not limited to indirect communication such as email and text messaging. Face-to-face is often far more disruptive. We may for example want to pop into a friend's house for just 15 minutes and end up spending hours, we often pass by a work colleague's desk and pause for a quick chat, ending up spending far longer than we should have and the rest of the day becomes a mad rush or a write off. The work place coffee machine is particularly bad for this sort of thing, so is the canteen or the smokers' corner. A few minutes of chatting often turns into tens of minutes, thirty minutes or even hours. I have helped large organisations with time management and it's always a fascinating exercise to ask staff to quietly write down how many minutes and hours they spent during the last week socialising at work. On average I would say over 10 hours a week are spent chatting on non-work related topics. This in itself is not a problem, after all, work is the biggest social event of your life. It does, however, become a problem when productivity suffers, when deadlines are not met, and when staff claim they don't have time to do all that needs to be done.

Not only do we actively seek out social interaction by checking our email, logging on to social networking sites and visiting friends, but we also fall victim to others who seek out social interaction. I am sure you can remember a time when you were doing something important at home and the doorbell rang. Standing outside was an unexpected visitor; a friend, a colleague or a neighbour. What starts as a two minute chat at the door ends over an hour later with both of you still standing at the door. Unexpected visitors can be a problem and it's not limited to our front door. A colleague who comes to our office and a friend we meet on the street, are all potential traps into which we may fall and end up chatting too long even though we are very busy.

Now don't get me wrong, in some cases it is important that these things happen. Reconnecting with a long lost friend on the street is very important, the worries of a work colleague may well be worth spending an extra hour on and of course building your links with your community is invaluable. However, at other times these situations can rob us of something far more important, forcing us to change our plans, make adjustments to the day's goals and, in some cases, write off entire days.

Spending time with friends, neighbours, family and work colleagues is good but we need to set boundaries or these times quickly spiral out of control. This is not as difficult as you may think. For example if you are planning to go out to dinner with a friend you can do one of two things; either set a time limit of two hours or plan to go out to dinner later in the evening. A dinner that starts at 8pm instead of 7pm gives you an extra hour to spend on something else, perhaps your children or to practice that musical instrument, or write that chapter of your book. One thing I find helps is to look at my watch before I begin any conversation.

even a short one at a colleague's desk. Knowing the time does two things: firstly, it helps me remember to keep it short and secondly, it helps me keep track of how much time I have really spent talking. Another way to avoid socialising from getting out of control is to tell the person at the beginning of the conversation how much time you have available. So for example if you are meeting for coffee, start with the sentence "Hi Jo, great to meet up but I only have thirty minutes before my next meeting." Short sentences like this go a long way to keeping things under control and are great for helping other people know that it's not them, it's you- you want to succeed.

Everyone is different, we all have different priorities and our schedules are all unique. Some of us can afford to spend hours with an acquaintance, others only have ten minutes. Whatever your situation, what is important is that you take the time to think about how you spend your energy and resources. Don't just let it flow, because inevitably it will flow endlessly and ultimately you will regret it. It is best to use some system to keep track of the time and resources we spend socialising. I have given just two examples above but there are countless ways to keep track of time. Whatever system you use, what is important is that you have a system and that you use it.

Trap No. 2: Fire Fighting

Fires are dangerous things. A few weeks ago we were rudely awoken in the early hours of the morning by the sound of a commotion outside our house. Three doors down from us a house had caught fire. The flames had blown out one of the windows and were starting to engulf the entire house when the fire fighters arrived. They quickly got to work with their hoses, axes and crow bars. Entering the house under the cover of water being dowsed on the fire from their colleagues, they proceeded to put the fire out from the inside. Within 10 or 15 minutes the fire seemed to be out. However, the fire fighters remained for another 3 hours while they systematically combed every inch of the house looking for any sign that the fire might start again. Whatever the fire did not destroy the fire fighters did. Not only did they drench the house with their water cannons, causing massive amounts of water damage, but they ripped the plasterboards off the walls and tore down the ceilings looking for any sparks. Everything that could be moved was unceremoniously dumped on the front lawn in a large, partially burnt and completely soaked pile of personal effects. There really was very little salvageable by the time the fire fighters had gone.

I remember, as I helped my neighbours sort through the pile of what was then nothing more than rubble, thinking to myself: what would I do if it was my house? I even remember going back home just a few hours later and taking a few moments to look around. I have always kept everything of importance in a single folder to be grabbed in such situations, but the reality of the fire just a few doors down made me rethink about what was really important. During that time my wife and I decided to never make things our life, never to be so attached to objects that we would be left defeated if they were destroyed.

Fires are not only dangerous because they can cause physical harm, and are life threatening; they are dangerous for a multitude of other reasons. They put our personal belongings, our life style and our future at risk. They are traumatic because they come upon us unexpectedly. No one plans for a fire. No one puts it in their diary and says "on Tuesday next week we are going to have a fire in our house." It's something that just happens. They are unpredictable and cannot be controlled. As a consequence, when they arise, they demand our immediate attention. We need to drop everything and deal with the fire at once. If we don't, our lives, belongings and future are at risk.

Of course fires are not only physical realities composed of hot flames. We often have unexpected troubles in our lives that demand our immediate attention or our lives, belongings and future will be at risk. These types of "fires" can take place anywhere and anytime. They can take place at work, at home, in the family, or even within ourselves as we struggle with our emotional well-being. At work it may take the form of a lost document, a sudden visit by the boss who wants to see a report on the progress of a key account, or a colleague who has misunderstood our instructions and made a mistake that needs to be sorted out immediately. At home, so my experience tells me, fires occur often. The washing machine breaks and floods the kitchen, a family member falls ill and ends up in hospital, the car breaks down, the children get in trouble at school and we need to speak to the headmaster, the dinner is burnt and we have to sort something out, the list goes on and on.

All these "fires" demand our immediate attention and cause us to shift our focus away from the general direction of a successful future to the specific and immediate crisis in our present. In principle there is nothing wrong with fighting these fires. These are, after all, important and urgent matters that need to be dealt with. However, it is possible that we spend our entire life fighting fires. In some cases these "fires" can consume everything we do and take up all of our time. They can become so numerous and so common that there is no time left in the day to accomplish anything else. As a result we never really achieve what we need to achieve now, and when the future comes around, that which should have been done in the present, becomes a fire that needs to be put out.

Let me give you an example. Say that we notice our son has failed a maths test. We know that he has the aptitude for maths and really should be doing better. However, when he brings us his maths test we are struggling to fix the washing machine and so decide to talk to him tomorrow about it. The next day we notice that the new washing machine we ordered is not right and we spend the whole day trying to rectify the mistake; calling the seller (who is impossible to reach), arranging the paperwork and getting a carrier to pick it up. Then of course we have to sort out dinner and the younger child needs a bit of attention because she has had a difficult day at play school and is moody, tearful and generally grumpy. Dinner burns, she cries, the wife is away on a conference and by the time we get the youngest to bed there is no time to talk to our son about his maths. There is always tomorrow we reason to ourselves. However, the next day is much like the first and we end up "fire fighting" the whole day. A few weeks pass by in much the same way until one day we get a letter from the school, our son has failed his maths exam, the school would like to keep him back and the teacher needs to talk to us urgently. What started as one failed test turns into a serious problem which now demands our immediate attention. The small spark we saw on the horizon has turned into a raging fire, not only for us but for our son as well.

This situation is quite common to many parents, indeed to many people who can relate to the feeling of being "out of control," the feeling of having to deal with whatever "fire" comes our way and lacking the opportunity to break the cycle. Yesterday's sparks are today's fires and today's sparks are the raging blazes of tomorrow. I have had the misfortune of meeting many people who spend their life "fire fighting." I can tell you that it is not a pretty sight; anxiety, stress, worry and most of all the overwhelming feeling of getting nowhere, drains the energy and life from them. They become slaves to situations, slaves to external influences and lose all hope of a future in which they are in control.

If fire fighting becomes the sum of our daily activities then our long-term lasting success will be compromised and we will find ourselves risking everything for the daily demands of our life. We need to break this cycle. No matter what we are faced with today we need to spend a small part of everyday taking the time to think things through thoroughly. We need to lift our heads above the flames we are fighting today, looking toward the horizon to see the sparks we will be fighting tomorrow. If, slowly, we can work on some of those sparks, putting them out before they become fires, we can begin to gain control. Every day may see a few less fires and this will give us time to put out a few more sparks. Soon we will rarely deal with fires and can have the satisfaction of spending a large portion of our energy and resources on what really matters. Consequently we will become more and more successful in the areas of our life that we know we should be succeeding at.

My advice is as follows: Firstly, it is imperative that we recognise the difference between "fire fighting" and true success. We need to know when we are just "fighting a fire" and when we are actually achieving something long-term and lasting. Secondly, the moment we notice that we are simply "fire fighting" we need to stop and take the time to think things through thoroughly, looking to the horizon. We need to ask ourselves the question: "what is the real consequence of not fighting this fire?" Will this fire really destroy us or is it perhaps something we need to fail at? Some fires burn themselves out (as is often the case with the unimportant but urgent matters of our lives) other fires ravage areas of our life that we don't really care about; so what if the TV is broken or the dinner we cook tonight is not perfect? Unless these things are central to your life's ambition, to what you believe is the most important thing in the universe, sometimes it's best to let these fires burn. Remember that a field is often renewed to a darker shade of green after a fire, in the same way, if letting a small fire burn helps us to take charge of the future, then our futures will be greener because of the fire that crossed our path today.

Thirdly, and most importantly, remember that Murphy is lurking everywhere. His law is often the cause of fires to come. Consider the sparks in your life now and ask yourself, "which one of these sparks is going to fane into a fire which I will need to fight tomorrow?" If at all possible try to squash the spark today so that the fire is prevented tomorrow. It may take a bit more energy than you think you have today, but my experience is that fighting a spark today takes far less energy than battling the blaze tomorrow. So take the time to think things through thoroughly today and save yourself the trouble and trauma of a fire tomorrow.

Trap No. 3: The Misplaced and Forgotten Things

There was an advert on the TV today for a car that has keyless entry. The advert plays on the common experience of looking for your car keys when you are running late or are out of time. One of the funniest scenes in the advert is a couple who had parked their car on a seaside jetty during low tide. As the tide has come in, the waters begin to rise and the car is now sitting in about a foot of water. They are arguing frantically with each other over who had the keys last as their car is being slowly engulfed by seawater.

Misplacing our car keys and only realising it when we are in a rush is so common that we cannot help but relate to the couple standing shin deep in sea water struggling to find their keys.

Of course this is not only limited to car keys. We have all misplaced documents at work and have been left with egg on our face when the boss or client asks us for the documents which should be easily at hand but are far from sight. We feel stupid as we rummage through the stacks of paper on our desk and the filing cabinet trying to find the important paperwork. Missing and losing something seems to be an experience for every age. Children misplace their homework all the time, adults their paperwork. It seems to be a fact of life that causes anxiety, stress, worry and takes up our time as we spend hours looking for our glasses, pen, wallet or that warrantee for the broken TV.

I have to say that my wife is particularly bad at this. I remember a few years ago, while we were still dating, we had planned to go on holiday to the Canary Islands. The cheapest flights always leave at six in the morning and so that evening each of us returned to our home to start packing. At about 11 o'clock in the evening I got a phone call from my wife who was panicking because she had lost her passport. She was searching everywhere but could not find it and wanted to know if I had it from our last trip. Of course I did not (it's very rare that the blame in these situations can be passed on to someone else). I headed over to her house and spent a few hours looking for it. Then I returned to my house and spent the rest of the night, all night, looking for it. We decided that if we did not find it by four in the morning we would cancel the trip. At five to four, while she had gone to sleep, her father- who clearly had taken the time to think things through thoroughly- had gone to the car and removed the glove box. The passport had fallen behind the glove box as my wife had thoughtlessly tossed it into the glove box at the end of the last trip. I wish I could say that that was the last time my wife lost an important document, even her passport, but alas, she has given me many fires over the years we have been together.

Another common error we make is to forget. We forget to pay the electricity bill, forget a meeting, a child's football game, a doctor's appointment, or to call our grandmother. Often, by the time we remember, the spark has turned into a fire and Murphy has taken full advantage of the situation. What could have been prevented with a little note somewhere is now a major issue and no amount of notes will solve it once it turns into a fire. An anniversary is forgotten and spent fighting with our spouse, the electricity cuts out and we are left in the dark, the meeting is missed and we are in trouble with our boss, our daughter's first music recital is lost and we have no memories or pictures.

It's important that we try to avoid these situations as often as possible. We need to take steps to prevent fires caused by misplaced and forgotten things. The first step is to know who you are. Go back to the beginning of this book and consider the chapter entitled: Know Thy Self. We are all people who forget and lose things. It should be always at the forefront of our minds whenever something important comes our way. When our child tells us of their upcoming football game we need to think to ourselves: "I am going to forget this-I need to write it down." If we have our passport in our hand, we need to be conscious of the fact that it is a very important document and losing it is going to cause major concerns. We need to know that we are likely to lose it and therefore need to take steps to ensure this does not happen. The most important factor in not losing or forgetting things is to know who you are, to know that you are going to lose and forget them. This knowledge is true power as it ensures that you take just a little more time to think things through thoroughly and to put structures in place that will help you remember where you left important items and to recall important information.

My advice is to have one place to put important things; for example on a shelf or in a drawer close to the front door. Make an unbreakable promise to yourself that if you can't pack something away where it goes (such as in your files or fire folder) that you will never leave it anywhere but that drawer or shelf. You will not put it in your bag, not on the kitchen table or leave it in the car. It will always be put in that drawer, placed on that shelf. This includes keys. If you can't put them back on the key holder then at least put them on that shelf or in that drawer. Make a promise with yourself that you will never tell yourself the lie "I will know where I left it" if you leave it somewhere else. This is an important, habit forming practice that has saved me literally hundreds of hours and mountains of stress.

Something either has its place (in my fire folder for example), or it goes on the shelf just as we come into our front door. For example, I have a pen which was given to me on a special occasion and that has great sentimental value to me. I know that it is likely to be lost and as a result I never take my pen away from my desk. Even if I can't find a pen anywhere else, I will go to my desk to use it when I need it, and will put it back where it belongs when I am finished. My wife knows that if she moves that pen from my desk then dark clouds will loom over our marriage, her husband will be turned into a monster and a fight is sure to follow.

Do not fool yourself into believing that you will remember. You will not remember that important date, that meeting, that appointment, to phone your friend, to call the doctor, or book the car in for a service. If you start lying to yourself and believing that you are the kind of person who will remember, you will become complacent and soon your memory will fade. You need to keep a diary, a to-do list, a folder, a piece of paper, a Dictaphone, anything to help you remember. Don't let anyone give you important information without you putting it somewhere. Today we have smart phones, these devices are perfect for this sort of thing; a note here and there, or an entry in our diary. I have a "to do" list in my calendar and make full use of the features on my expensive phone (of course cheaper phones will work just as well). Whatever system you have, it is important to use it. Know yourself, don't lie to yourself; you will forget, you need something to remind you.

Trap No. 4: The 10 Percent Rule

Napoleon Hill wrote a book many decades ago entitled *Think and Grow Rich*. In it he investigated some of the key principles that have helped to shape the success of many of the CEO's of fortune 500 companies. While reading this book I was fascinated and captivated by a principle which has subsequently become known to me as the 10 percent rule. Now, there are many of these 10 percent rules that I have come across but the one that is effective for personal success and development is known by this definition: "whenever you get tired and feel you cannot do more, push hard for 10 percent more."

The rule is well known to athletes (although they may not know it by this name). Take for example the body builder who goes to the gym. They will begin their work-out and start to lift weights. At the beginning of their session the work they do has very little benefit to their goal of building more muscles. They are fresh and hardly tired and so the body can easily lift the weights they use without needing to strain itself to promote muscle growth. However, after a while they begin to get tired and begin to feel the strain of the weights. A good body builder knows that when they feel they have reached their limit they need to push just a little harder. It is in this little extra that the benefit is found. When they can do no more, that is when their workout begins. By pushing just a little more and working just a little harder, the body struggles to cope with its current muscle strength. As a result it initiates the process of muscle development both in terms of growing new muscle and in strengthening the current muscle. They may have done a hundred bicep curls but it's the last 10 that made all the difference. The other 90 were just working up to that last set of 10.

The principle is the same for almost any other area of life, not only do most athletes work on this principle; runners push harder in the end, gymnast flex until it hurts then push a little more, sales people know that pushing a sale just a little after the first "no" translates into far more sales, students know that a little extra revision means a better mark and, while people often forget, a little extra effort in your relationships will result in deeper, stronger, and healthier bonds.

The key to experiencing more success than you do at the moment is not to double your efforts; this would be unreasonable. It would be impossible, for many of us, to do twice as much as we do at the moment. The key is to do just a little more than you feel you can do. To push just a little harder, especially when you feel you cannot push any more. The trick is not to do more than is humanly possible, the trick is to do just a little more than you feel you can do. This helps to ensure that you are doing the best you can, and increases the chances of success in your chosen field in three ways. Firstly, you are doing more work and often, not always, but often, more work translates into greater rewards.

Secondly, by doing just a little more than you can do, you counter the effect of the times that you can't do anything. If you recall back to previous sections; some days are simply written off. This is not in itself problematic. However, we need to overcome this by doing as much as we can on the days which are productive. By doing more on these days we counter the loss experienced during days we have had to write off. Thirdly, it is far easier to motivate yourself to do a little more than to double your efforts. Therefore, when you are almost about to stop because you cannot go further, it's easier to motivate yourself to do just a few more push-ups, spend a few more minutes at the desk, or a little longer at the musical instrument, than to do a whole lot more. Where there is motivation there is action and when motivation is maximized, action is maximised. Increased motivation translates into increased action.

The 10 percent rule applies to almost every aspect of life. If you want to lose some weight eat just a little healthier and do just a little bit more exercise. If you want to learn a new language just spend a little longer practicing the vocabulary and grammar, if you want to play the guitar and your fingers are hurting just do a little more, if you want to get that promotion at work just work a little harder than you are now, push to what feels like your full capacity and then push a little more. It is this 10 percent that separates the "good" from the "poor", the "better" from the "good" and the "best" from the "better."

Trap No. 5: Practice Failing

Often the key to success is to practice. This was something our grandparents taught us. "Practice makes perfect." Yet this basic lesson may seem at odds with our current culture which seeks instant success, instant results. Even in our workplace it has become common to expect a new employee to get it right with very little practice, or for students to learn without the need for repetition (repetition almost seems antithetical in our current "modern" education system). Nevertheless, there is simply no getting around it. If you want to be good at something, experience and practice are important and the same applies to conscious failure.

Habits are your mind's way of saving time. The mind is generally lazy and as a result it forms habits which are directly linked to the physical neurological pathways of your brain. By not having to think about everything, your mind can take the time to think about what it thinks are important things. So for example try this: fold your arms, now unfold them, now fold them again. Without thinking you would have folded your arms the same way as before. Almost everyone folds their arms in the same way every time they fold their arms. The same is true for the way you brush your teeth. We always start on the same side, in the same way. If we are used to putting on our left shoe first we will do it every day without thinking.

I have been told that if you wanted to change the way you fold your arms, say right over left instead of left over right, it would take 21 days for new synaptic pathways to be formed. Although I am not a neurological specialist, I do believe this information to be true because I have tried it. Indeed it takes about three weeks to form (or break) a habit. This includes the habit of washing the dishes while you cook, cleaning the shower when you step out of it, putting on your right sock first instead of your left and of course, the habit of failing when you want to succeed.

If you want to learn to fail, want to make a habit of failing in unimportant things, it will take a little time and you have to practice it. This means you have to experience the process of failing, making the decision to fail, the act of failure and the consequences. You need to make it such an integral part of your life that you no longer think about it, like a musician playing the piano, failing must come naturally to you and the only true way of ensuring this is to practice. Practice failure and it will become natural.

Now at first this may seem at odds with everything you have been brought up to believe. After all, we are all taught to try to be successful. We are taught to try and not let people down, to do all we can, to look out for our friends in all things, to say "yes" when people ask us to do things. The very notion of consciously failing at something is alien to us; it seems at odds with the concept of success. After all, how can I be a success if I am always failing? Because of this deep ingrained desire to succeed at everything, we struggle to fail at the unimportant things. We need to practice failing so that it becomes as much a part of the way we think as success is.

The steps are relatively simple and I have found that the process is not as difficult as one might imagine. Firstly, one needs to make a habit of thinking things through thoroughly. This is the first and most important step to both success and failure. How we think about what we do, determines what and how we achieve it. Getting into a habit of thinking about things clearly and thoroughly is therefore very important. While this may take a bit of effort, it really does not take much more time. After all, your mind is very quick and one can take a second to question something, to stop and look at what we are doing and, most importantly, why we are doing it. So make this the first step.

Secondly, and perhaps far more difficultly, we need to practice the actual act of failing. Once you have learnt to question everything you do and have developed a habit of thinking about what you do, the next step is to choose to fail at some things. You need to choose to fail at something every day. Say for example; not cleaning a dish. Just leave it out one day. Don't mow the lawn, let it grow. Choose not to make your bed, leave it a mess. Don't wash the car or iron a shirt. Do something every day that feels wrong to you. Choose to fail at it and make the conscious decision to do so.

Of course, it is important that you choose to succeed at something else at the same time. So for example if you don't mow the lawn, then spend the time learning a new skill (playing the guitar or learning Mongolian). If you don't take the car to be washed then take the children to get an ice-cream instead. If you don't do the dishes then, perhaps, take 10 minutes to wash a few windows. The point is not to be lazy. We are not failing so that we can sit around and do nothing. We are choosing to fail so that we can do something more important. It is vital that we choose success as we practice to fail. On the one hand we need to practice failure, on the other hand we need to practice success in important areas.

My advice is to start small, have a bit of fun with the things you know are not that important, the dishes, the lawn, the shower etc. When you see the benefits in other areas (such as closer relationships with your family, more fluency in that language, better financial planning in your budget etc.) then move on to some more serious things such as saying "no" to a friend, or failing at something you really feel you must do but know is not important. Start small and build it up but whatever you do, you need to practice failing, you need to make it as much a part of your life as your desire to succeed. So before you move on to the next section; take the time to think things through thoroughly today and choose to fail at something right now.

Chapter 12: Do the Right Thing, the Hard Thing and the Great Thing

Quite a while ago, when I was still in my first year at university, we received a lecture on principles to help make tough choices in life. I will never forget the well-known story the speaker told about two friends. One was a king and the other was soon to be. These friends were at war with each other. The king wrongly believed that his friend was trying to steal his thrown and so he had mobilised his army and was chasing his friend. His friend fled to the mountains and was hiding in some caves. Of course the king followed him and brought his army to the mountains. One day the king and his army were camped on the foothill of a mountain. He too found some caves and used them as shelter. What he did not know, however, was the cave he had chosen was the very same cave his friend had chosen.

While the king slept his friend looked at him and thought long and hard about what to do. He could kill the king and thus stop the king from chasing and killing him. Or he could let the king live, after all, the king was his friend. It was a tough choice and one which took the entire night to decide. Very early in the morning, before the king had woken up, the king's friend snuck up to the king's bed and cut off a piece of his cloak. Then he returned to his hiding place deep within the cave. When the sun rose the king got up and continued with the business of the day, chasing what he thought was a traitor. When the king's camp had packed up and was ready to leave, the king's friend stood a little distance up the mountain and shouted his greetings to the king. Naturally the king was surprised, but before he could send his soldiers in to kill the traitor, the king's friend held up a piece of his cloak and explained to the king that he could have killed him in the night but chose not to because he was actually the king's friend and had no intention of harming the king. The king was shocked and stunned, he suddenly realised how foolish he had been. He sent his army home and returned to his castle leaving his friend in peace. When the king died, his friend became the new king and to this day is considered the greatest king that nation ever had.

I have always loved this story and found it remarkable how the friend spares the king's life even though the king had been chasing him with the sole intent to kill him. Did the friend know that the king would give up once he saw the truth? Did he ever really consider killing his king? What went through his mind at the back of the cave while he watched the king sleep and how was it that he was able to come up with such a wise solution? The lecturer explained to us that we can draw three principles from this story that can help us make tough choices. These three principles have stuck with me ever since and have truly guided me through some tough times in my life.

Do the Right Thing

The first principle we learn from this story is that we should try as hard as possible to do the right thing. The friend could have killed the king silently in the night then slipped away. He would have been rid of the king and the army would have disbanded and left him in peace. He would have been free and possibly, if he played his cards right, could have even been king much sooner. However, this would mean killing his friend and his king. Killing his friend would have been the wrong thing; it goes against all the laws of friendship and flies in the face of what it means to be someone's friend. It would also mean killing his king, the person to which he had sworn allegiance, the person who, at that time, it was believed God had appointed to rule. Killing the king meant going against everything society stood for, law, order, loyalty and service. It was simply the wrong thing to do.

What has always struck me about the friend is that he did not do the right thing for himself; he did the right thing-full stop. Whenever I encourage people to do the right thing they inevitably get the message: do the right thing for you. This, however, is not what I mean. I mean do the right thing, not the right thing for you. While it is possible that these two may be synonymous at times, often doing the right thing does not mean doing the right thing for yourself, quite the contrary, I am afraid. Often it means that you will suffer and that someone else will benefit.

Let me give you an example, marriage today has been eroded by this concept of do the right thing, and by that we mean: do what makes YOU happy. When people are told to do the right thing in marriage, they often hear the message: make yourself happy. The end result is often divorce and family breakup. However, it is often the case that doing the right thing means that you have to change your ways, apologise for the pain you have caused, forgive and love your partner in spite of the pain they have caused you. While it is true that sometimes divorce seems to be the better option, this is, in the most part, not the case. A change of heart, an act of humility and a spirit of service can often reshape a marriage and save a family.

The same is often true of our work lives. We are often

wronged, often hurt and often feel that we have been misunderstood and treated unfairly at work. Doing the right thing may mean two different things. On the one hand it may mean doing the right thing for you, quit your job, resign your post and seek work elsewhere, but what does this mean for your family or for your work colleagues? How do you change a bad work environment if you give up and run away? You may feel that you have a right to quit, but does that mean it is the right thing to do? Does it mean we demand our rights and force others into positions they don't want to be in; or make life difficult for ourselves, our family, or our colleagues so that we may secure what we feel entitled too? Or does it perhaps mean fighting for the rights of others, giving up our own rights so that our family may be happier, supporting a work colleague through a hard time or even sticking with a job so that we can press forward with our career and achieve our life's ambitions?

While there are such things as universal rights and wrongs, and here I must disagree with the tenets of post-modernism, often it is difficult to know what these rights and wrongs are. Killing a friend is wrong, stealing from your workplace is unethical, cheating on your wife is unacceptable. In some cases the right thing is easy to identify, in other cases it is not so obvious.

This is why we need to take the time to think things through thoroughly. Taking your time to think about the choices you make will, in the long run, pay off. Thinking clearly about what is right and wrong, or at least more right and less wrong, in your situation will help you to make better decisions. It is in ambiguous situations that your guiding principle is particularly important. When you struggle to see what is right and what is wrong, your guiding principle, the direction you want your life to take, might shed some light on your decision and help to give you direction.

So when faced with a tough decision the first thing to do is to take the time to think things through thoroughly in light of what is the most important thing in the universe that never changes. Make your decisions based on this; on what is always right and not what's right for you now.

Do the Hard Thing

Doing the right thing can be hard; there is no getting around it. In fact, it is my experience (and the experience of millions of others), that the hard thing is often the right thing. Of course this is not always the case, but as a general rule, doing the right thing is harder than doing the wrong thing. Quitting your job is often easier than fighting for what's right. Getting divorced may seem easier (although it is often tougher) than fighting through the difficult times. Spending time with your family takes far more energy than watching your favourite TV show.

It is in doing the right thing that the truly successful person excels. Not only are they able to overcome their natural inclination to find the easiest, quickest route to a life of luxury, but they have the vision to see that life of luxury for what it really is; a false reality, a reality that ultimately is not truly successful. Being happy for example may mean eating fast food every day and doing nothing but watching TV on the sofa. That may at first seem like a life filled with luxury, and therefore success; after all, you have spent your life enjoying yourself. However, on closer inspection it soon becomes apparent that you have wasted your life and that ultimately you will not be content. While this simple example may at first seem obvious, the basic principle applies to more ambiguous situations.

I once knew a young man, in his mid-twenties. He had just gotten married and had had twin girls. His wife could not work and raise the children. He was well qualified in IT and had obtained a job with flexible hours that allowed him to work from home. He had moved into the countryside where life was a little cheaper. This worked well for the first six months but life was not easy because their finances were stretched. This young man decided to quit his job and get a job in the city earning almost double his salary. He could no longer work from home or have flexible hours in the new job, but the salary was far better and he longed to have more money. The new job meant that he had to leave the house at six in the morning and return home at seven at night. While he had far more disposable income than before, he had far less time to spent with his family. Being gone for more than 12 hours a day and being tired and stressed on returning home, took a toll on his family life. The marriage suffered, the children suffered, he suffered himself but he was wealthier.

The general success of this young man's decision rests on his driving principle, his ultimate goal in life. If the most important thing for this young man was money, then we can conclude that he was indeed right to pick the job in the city. However, if his main goal was to spend time with his family and to enjoy the benefits of being both a father and a husband, then he could hardly be called successful. Money does not equate to success, much in the same way as "happier" does not mean "better." Often the hard thing is the right thing. If this young man saw success as spending time with his family, then he should have struggled through his financial concerns and enjoyed the benefits of having a job that provided the flexibility to spend as much time as he could with his new wife and baby girls. A new car, branded cloths, foreign holidays and the best food are not worth the price of a family.

When faced with a tough choice, a difficult situation or a hard road ahead, we need to take the time to think things through thoroughly and decide on the right way forward. My advice is to lean toward the harder option. While it is true that the harder option is not always the right option, and one should never choose it simply because it is hard, it is often the case that it is hard because it is right and doing the right thing often means doing the hard thing. Consequently one may say that doing the right thing is hard, that is what makes it the "great thing."

Do the Great Thing

Even though doing the right thing is often the hardest option available, it frequently has the greatest benefits and this makes it the great thing. Greatness is something we all strive for, it is built into our biology, it's a part of our DNA. We all want to be great, great at something, maybe even great at everything. We want to climb Mount Everest, want to win an Olympic gold medal, write a prizewinning book, want to be the best dad in the world. The problem is that these things are not easy. This is why we look up to those who do them and consequently why we believe them to be great. It's hard to train for the Olympics, hard to sit down and write, hard to spend time with screaming, crying, messy children and hard to put in the hours, energy and resources necessary to start our own fortune 500 company.

Great things take time, effort, energy, resources and often sacrifice. These sacrifices are, in almost all cases, severe. To go to the Olympics one needs to train every day, spending hours upon hours at your sport. It's tiring, hard, frustrating and the chances of success; winning a gold medal, are often against you. It requires discipline, dedication and perseverance, but above all, it requires that we give up what we are naturally inclined to reach out for; a simple, easy life. Talent only goes so far when it comes to the

Olympics and as a rule I would say that it is not the most talented who win gold but the most dedicated, those who work the hardest. Talent brings us to the starting line, hard work to the finishing line.

This is why we admire those who have achieved great things; because it took so much to attain. We look up to them, hail them as heroes, put them on the cover of our magazines, interview them on TV, write books about them. We tell our children to be like them as our parents told us to follow their example. We consider them great; it's ingrained in our very being, there in the very essence of humanity.

True, lasting success must have some form of greatness attached. It is simply impossible to be a truly successful person without some element of greatness. It does not matter if we are talking about success in business, sports, family or even personal success. If there is no greatness in it, there is no true success- it will bring no contentment. As colour is to flowers, so is greatness to success.

The key to greatness is not to follow it for its own sake. One should not strive to be great for the sake of greatness. Such an understanding of life seems to be at the root of our celebrity culture. We want to be famous for the sake of fame. This kind of thinking does not lead to greatness but rather to following the easy and often wrong path. An athlete does not strive to win a gold medal because she wants to be honoured and famed. She strives to be the best she can be, to achieve the highest level of success in her chosen sport. She takes her talent, looks far into the future and asks herself: "what's the most I can make of this gift?" Through hard work and dedication she strives to develop her talent, and the perfecting of the talent is in itself the end goal. An athlete who strives for the gold medal alone will find the medal empty and worthless. She will stand on the podium and know that she did not do her best and that she could have done better. Where is the greatness in an Olympic gold medal given to second best?

This applies to many other areas of our life. What is the point of being a great father if we could be a better one, a great businessperson if we have only given a minimum of effort? The same is true for being a great friend, a great son, a great doctor, lawyer, engineer or street sweeper. We will never be great people if we do not first strive to do what is right and then to follow this path through the hard work to the reward of being great at something.

To be great one needs not strive for greatness in itself, but rather to follow the route of doing the right thing, putting in the hard work and then achieving greatness. There is no other way to greatness than following these two steps first. One must do what is right and what is hard before one achieves true greatness. Since "greatness" follows "difficulty" and "difficulty" follows taking the right path in life, the three are intimately entwined. To be successful means doing the right, the hard and the great thing. Our life's goal, the most important thing in the universe that never changes, should be the right thing, the hard thing, the great thing.

Chapter 13: Plotting the Trajectory to Success

It is widely accepted that a lack of planning is the number one reason for failure. Often someone will have a deep desire to reach for their goals, to achieve lasting success and yet they fail to put in place any plan of action. As a result they aimlessly wander through life, doing what needs to be done, when it needs to be done, without any direction. The end result is that they miss their goals and in most cases they end up a long way off. Knowing what you want to achieve is one thing, but putting in place a plan of action is another, altogether different matter.

The importance of planning cannot be understated. A plan gives us the tools to succeed; it paints a road map for us to travel along and provides the opportunity to monitor our journey, thereby making necessary corrections as the journey progresses. Without this map there is almost no chance of reaching our destination (achieving our life's goals and experiencing real, long-term success). Since the importance of planning is well understood, one would be forgiven for thinking that it is something we teach our children. However, this simply is not the case. The school system, to the best of my knowledge, has no real curriculum on the matter. There is no course, class or lecture that deals with the topic: how do you plan to succeed?

I act as one of the governors for a local community secondary school. A few months ago I attended a conference at the school where teachers, parents and governors could get together to decide what was best for the children of the school and to produce a strategy to achieve this. I was at a table with some teachers and a parent. One of the teachers was the head of one of the departments. There was a lot of discussion about what we hoped for the children of the school. The overwhelming consensus was that we wanted the children to be successful. What I found strange, however, was that there was no real concept of success or even of how to get the children to reach it. Rather, the teachers felt that they knew what success meant for every child and they would work to help the child reach this expectation. I urged the teachers to teach the children two key skills; firstly to teach them how to choose valuable goals for their life and secondly to teach them how to be successful at reaching those goals. My argument is as follows. If the student does not choose the goals themselves, then the goals they reach are not their own goals but the goals of the teacher. Consequently, if success means to reach your own goal, then in this case, it is not the student who is successful but the teacher.

In short the message was clear from the school. Teachers know best what the child can and should achieve. It is the teachers who will set the goals and the teachers who will put in place the steps necessary for the children to reach those gaols. Our schools do not teach children how to choose their own goals, what principles to use to decide a direction in life, and the basic process of making life-guiding decisions. More than this, our schools fail to teach our children how to develop and put in place a basic plan for reaching their own goals. Our children leave school, their heads full of facts and figures. They have the skills necessary to go to college, to get jobs and to contribute to our tax system but the skills to be truly successful elude them.

The more people I interact with, the more people I help, the more I am convinced that this is the case. The basics of planning elude most people. It is not that most people are stupid, or that they are lazy, it is often simply not their fault. It is the consequence of their up-bringing, the schools they went to and the education they received.

Let me ask you a question I have asked thousands of other people: what information do you need in order to get to a destination? Say you were going to London. What do you need to know to get there? Pause if you will and think about this simple question for just one minute.

When I pose this question to participants of my seminars they inevitably come up with two bits of information. I need to know where London is (where I am going) and I need to know how to get there. At first this logic seems sound and you yourself may agree. However, a fundamentally important bit of information is missing from this equation. A piece of information so vital, that if it is not clearly understood, there is almost no hope of ever getting to London. Sometimes I can spend up to thirty minutes trying to draw this information out of a group of people I am helping. At first what is missing does not seem obvious, what else could possibly be needed? By now I hope you, the reader, have understood what is missing. If not, do pause now for just a few seconds and try to figure it out.

Perhaps the example of a car's satellite navigation system may be useful. Say I wanted to go to Las Vegas. I turn my car's satellite navigation system on and enter the destination as Las Vegas, but before the navigation system can plan a route it first calculates where I am. My current position, where am I now. This is vital to the process of planning a route to Las Vegas. While the destination may remain the same, the route will change depending on where I am. If I am in New York for example, the route will be completely different than if I am in San Francisco. To get anywhere in life I need these three bits of information: where am I, where am I going and what do I need to do to get there.

Where am I?

The first piece of information I need to create a plan that will help me to achieve my goals, is where am I? Naturally, in terms of life goals, this is not usually a geographical place, although of course it may be. This means I need to understand who I am (dealt with in the chapter: "Know Thy Self"), what I am like, my strengths, my weaknesses, my hopes and my dreams. I need to know my current skill set; what can I do and what skills I lack. This means considering what courses I have taken and what qualifications I have gained, however it also means thinking about what skills I have that I may not be officially qualified for. For example, I may be a good public speaker, or good at listening to people. There are very few pieces of paper that qualify someone to be a good mother or a great friend. I also need to think about the physical environment I inhabit, both internally and externally. What is my health like? Do I have weak knees, a bad back, poor eyesight? What about my external environment; what finances do I have, what assets do I own, where do I live geographically (is it a city or in the country and what country?).

What about my nationality? This affects both my internal and external context. Internally it affects my culture. On the one hand my culture could be conservative, I could be shy and quiet or on the other hand my culture could be boisterous, loud and extraverted. My nationality also effects my external environment. If I am a U.S. citizen I may struggle to emmigrate to Germany, whereas if I am an E.U citizen I can live and work freely in

Europe.

Knowing where I am will help me to plot out my path to success and it is for this reason that I have dedicated an entire chapter to the topic of knowing yourself. I encourage you, as I do throughout this book, to take the time to think things through thoroughly and get to know yourself. Really think about who you are, your skills, your deepest desires, your darkest fears, your hopes and ambitions. This knowledge will give you the power to choose a direction in life that best fits who you are.

Where am I Going?

The next bit of information I need to know is where am I going? Someone once said: if you don't know where you are going, you will always end up somewhere else. These words are so true. If we do not head in a direction, do not choose our destination, we will find that life takes us on a path that leads somewhere and there is a good chance we would prefer not to be there when we get there. Knowing where we are going is the bearing, the heading of our life and it is the central topic of this book. If you have a clear understanding of where you are going you can determine your direction and take measures to ensure that you get there.

While knowing where you are going is vital, it is pointless if it is not thought through. So many people choose to head in a direction without really thinking about it. They want to be famous, want to make money, want to have a beautiful wife, two children and a white picket fenced house. They don't really think about the consequences of going in this direction and, more importantly, reaching this destination. It is no wonder that mid-life crises are so common as men and women reach a point in their life where they realise they don't want to be where they are.

Getting a good job is fine, but what do you do when you get that job? Having children is great, but what will you do with them when you have them, when you need to make decisions for them first and you second?

We need to take the time to think things through thoroughly so that we have a clear understanding of what the most important thing to us is and how this will affect where we are going. It is not incidental that I mention this central idea again and again throughout this book, that I dedicate an entire chapter to it and that I urge you to take a long time to clearly think about what is important in life. Just because you have money, power and fame does not make you successful. In fact, some of the most unsuccessful people in the world had these things: think of Hitler, Stalin, Napoleon, Mussolini. All are considered failures by both our standards and their own (they even failed to reach their own goals).

I find that it helps to develop clear pictures in my head. This works for both my long-term and short-term goals. I often dream about my future just before I fall asleep at night. Where will I be living, what house will I be living in, what job will I be doing, what will my wife be like, my family, who will I be helping, how much money will I be making, what will I be doing with this money? It also works with my short-term goals. Say I want to start a new project; I see myself initiating it, running it, doing the administration, see the people I will help, the lives I will change, the impact I will make. A clear vision of where you are going helps to solidify the plan, gives it substance and helps your mind to make plans to achieve it.

What Do I Need to Do to Get There?

The last bit of information I need before I can make my plan is: what do I need to do to get there? Once I have clearly understood where I am and where I am going, I can connect the dots. If I want to drive a sports car but am currently driving an old beat up VW Beatle, I need to get a job that helps me earn enough money to sell my car and buy the sports car I want. If I want to be a doctor and I have just completed school then I need to enter university, if I have no schooling, then I need to go back and finish my schooling.

This part of planning changes for everyone and often needs adjusting during the course of our life. As our present situations change, we get blown off course and the regular events of life cause us to make adjustments to our plan. Nevertheless, if our destination stays the same and we stop and retake stock, we can, at any point, ask ourselves: where are we, where are we going and what do we need to do to get there.

My advice when thinking about what you need to do to reach your goal is to speak to someone else. This may be a friend, a family member or your life partner. Ask them what they think about your assessment of where you are and where you are going. Ask them if they can help you plot out a course to get there. This is something business managers are doing all the time. They almost never create plans for their section, divisions or company on their own. We are, as human beings, too prone to see the situation one way, to be boxed in by our own perceptions and to fail to see other options or the problems with our plans or the challenges that might lie ahead. It's always best to work within a team; a work place team, a family team or even a friendship team. This is why I think it's so important that human beings are not alone. It's good to have friends, good to get married, good to start families.

Before we move on I just want to give some final thoughts on planning. Firstly, nobody is an island. We all live in a world with other people. We have work colleagues, friends and family. Going somewhere is only really meaningful if you take someone with you. As a parent it is ultimately contrary to the ethos of family to make plans on your own. We can't decide the direction we are going in life if we don't take into account the opinions, ideas and thoughts of those who are in the same boat as us. We may be the captain of the vessel, may be making the most money in the family, have the highest education, the most promising career, or the strongest will, but if we force others to come along with us against what they want for their lives, they will ultimately resent us and we risk their success. Teams, workforces, friends and families need to decide together where they are, where they are going and what they need to do to get there.

Secondly, planning to succeed is not something you can do once and never do again. This simply is not possible. As life happens, our plans are bound to go astray. We will inevitably hit bumps along the way. Some of these bumps may be positive; for example, we are given the opportunity to take a great trip which costs us a some money which we may need to make up for later, we are offered a great job that will expand our horizons and will not ultimately jeopardise our entire life's direction, or we have a child which brings a lot of happiness into our lives but forces us to turn our focus away from our life's goal for a while. Other bumps may be unfortunate, we fall ill, the economy takes a turn for the worse, we lose our job or our house is flooded.

These diversions are going to affect your life's plan. The course you plot will change along the way and if you fail to take stock of where you are as you progress along the path, your plan will become unworkable. You need to continually stop and re-plan, continually ask yourself where are you, where are you going and what do you need to do to get there. Evaluating your progress against your long-term plan is something I recommend you do every three to four months at least. It may be, when you stop to evaluate, that you are still on the path you originally set and you can just continue doing what you have always been doing. It may be that you are no longer on track and you need to adjust your plan slightly or even drastically. Either way it's best to evaluate often. This will save you from going drastically off course and ensure that, on the whole, over the course of your life, you stay on track.

Finally, have these three questions ingrained into your very being. Continually ask yourself where are you, where are you going and what do you need to do to get there. These questions will help you with a wide range of situations, not just long-term life planning. They will help you with the little things, such as cooking dinner. For example, say you want steak for dinner (where are you going), you may look in the fridge (where are you), if there is no steak in the fridge then you may need to pop out and buy some (how do you get there). These three questions also help with more important problems. Say you are in the middle of an argument with your spouse. You may stop and think about what is going on, why are you arguing, what is happening right now (where am I), you may then think about what you want, the happy relationship you are seeking, a peaceful resolution to this situation (where am I going). It may then become easy to join the dots, what do you need to say and do to bring the two of you from where you are to where you want to be (what do I need to do to get there).

These three basic questions apply to getting a job, decorating the house, bringing up children, completing your studies, even tidying your room. Try to practice using them in both the mundane as well as the extraordinary activities you face. Get up in the morning and take 30 seconds to plan your day, take 10 seconds to plan your breakfast, 1 minute to plan to solve an argument. Continually use this system until it becomes second nature to you and in the end you will find that on the whole, your life starts to move towards the goals you are hoping to achieve.

Chapter 14: Some Final Thoughts

Control VS Influence

We all want to be in control. We want to take control of ourselves, our environment, and the people around us. Of course, deep down inside us we know that this is an illusion. We have some control but ultimately control rests in forces far beyond us. We may be able to control what we eat for breakfast, the clothes we wear, the makeup we put on. We may even exercise some control over the larger facts of our life; the house we live in, the car we drive, the person we marry (within reason of course).

Then there are the things we have no control over. The economy, the gender of our children, the weather, the traffic, or other people. Some of these things will make very little difference to our lives. If we work from home it does not really matter if it rains or shines. However, other aspects may make a big difference. If the economy takes a turn for the worse, as it has in the past, we may find ourselves out of a job. It may be difficult to make ends meet. If we fall ill through no fault of our own, we will have to struggle through the consequences. These events can severely impact our life's direction. We may be forced to quit the job we love, may be forced to take a break from a career, to move to a different location, do a different job and make new plans.

I have learnt that while I have control over the smaller things in my life, I exercise very little control over the larger aspects. This does not mean to say that I have absolutely no control. On the contrary, the choices I make and the decisions I take do have an impact on the general direction of my life. However, I would not call this control so much as influence. To control means to determine the outcome in such a way that it is a certainty. It is to ensure that what you want and desire does indeed transpire. Influence, on the other hand, is to guide, to impact, or to direct certain aspects of your life, choices and decisions in such a way as to make your desired outcome more likely. In the case of influence, your life's goals and ambitions are strong possibilities rather than certain outcomes.

There is no denying that there are certain advantages to having control. It is nice to know that you are secure and that your dreams and desires are going to come true. On the other hand there are certain advantages to having only influence and not control. The knowledge of how your life is going to turn out robs us of the mystery that is so important to the joy of life. Part of what makes life so enjoyable is the twist and turns that take place along the way; the strangers we never expected to change our lives, the surprises that help us experience things we never thought we would. Having control ensures we get what we want, but have you ever heard the saying: be careful what you wish for? A lot of the time I have been grateful that I have not gotten what I wanted. It's only in hindsight that we realise we did not really want what we worked so hard for. Sometimes, quite frequently in fact, the surprises turn out better than what we had originally planned.

In control there is no challenge but to control. When we try to control every aspect of our life we find that we are exerting our energy on wrestling control from forces that are far greater than us, rather than on our actual goals. We spend our lives fighting for control rather than fighting for what we want. At first this may seem to be one and the same thing, but on closer inspection we realise that we were fighting for the details and forgetting the bigger picture. For example, we fight to buy a certain house, to get a certain mortgage, to be accepted for a certain job, all the while not really fighting for a home, financial security or a meaningful career. Having control and reaching our goals are not always the same thing.

If we are in control, once we have wrestled it from the hands of our environment and those around us, we soon find that the challenge we so enjoy in achieving our goals is no longer there. Once I am in control, I no longer have any doubt as to the outcome, the activity itself becomes easy, the outcome assured and with the loss of challenge goes any sense of achievement. Why be proud, why be content, to have achieved the inevitable? Once we understand this, we realise that control is an illusion that robs us of the joy of life and the sense of adventure that is inherent in any successful venture.

Rather than wrestling for control all the time, my advice is to give up any fight for control in and for itself. Focus rather on influencing the outcomes of your life, on having an input in the general direction your life will take. Stop trying to ensure these outcomes and rather fight for them, stop trying to force the world around you to conform to your will, and simply try to convince it. The difference may seem subtle but it is important. On the one hand my energy is expended on gaining control, on the other hand my energy is spent on being successful in what I believe to be most important.

One key fact that will help you focus on influence rather than control is to shield yourself against things that are out of your control. At first you may say this is impossible, but the truth is you do it every day. For example you buy car insurance just in case someone else crashes into your car. The insurance insulates you from what might happen. Of course it does not fully protect you, but rather ensures that when things happen you are not irreparably thrown off course. Things can happen to anyone at any time and therefore it is important that we pick life goals that are in a certain sense insulated from unexpected events. So for example, try not to pick a life goal that focuses on one specific job or career. It would not be good to say that my life's goal is to fly an F-16 fighter jet. There are just too many things that can go wrong with this life goal. It may be that they stop making these jets, you may have bad eyesight, be too tall or too short, fail an entrance exam, have an accident or fall ill all of which may prevent you from flying this specific jet. Ultimately, even if you are successful and do become a fighter pilot for this type of plane, you can only do this for a certain period of time. Eventually you will get too old and you will have to retire. What will you do then?

Having life goals that are based more on principles and directions help us to be content and successful in a broad range of situations. So for example, one may say that their life's ambition is to protect their country. In this case there are many ways you can do this. Flying an F-16 fighter jet is just one way; other ways include supporting the troops, driving a supply vehicle, being a mechanic on a plane or an engineer in the army. While you may prefer to fly an F-16 fighter jet and may work towards achieving this goal. Ultimately whether you do or do not achieve this preference will not impact on your success. You will still be successful as long as you are working to protect your country.

This is why I encourage you throughout this book to answer the question: "what is the most important thing in the universe that will never change?" The "never change" part is vital to your life's goals. Our health changes, the economy changes, our family changes, and our appearance changes. Building our life on these things is dangerous and is a sure way to fail. Things outside of our control will impact on our goals and ensure failure as we try to cling to what is ultimately in a state of flux. It's a bit like trying to hold a boat steady in the middle of a storm; pointless and ultimately futile.

Of course this does not mean to say that we settle for anything. Far from it! We need to head in a general direction. We may not have control but we do have influence. We can make decisions and choices that will help to push us in certain directions. Both directly and indirectly, the choices we make will shape our lives. Exerting time and energy in helping to give our lives a good direction is hardly a waste. On the contrary it is perhaps the best use of our resources.

If we are to spend our time, energy and resources wisely, in the pursuit of success, we need to give up the fight for control and take up the battle for influence. We need to allow life to do what it does best; move on. We need to ride the river that is our life, moving with the changes, the ebb and flow. Rowing upstream against a raging river is almost impossible, however that does not mean we cannot navigate the river and choose a better path. While we need to put a rudder in the water and an oar to the side, we must resist the urge to row upstream. We should use the force of the river of life to take us down stream along a path of our influence. Where the river forks we can use our rudder (the visions and goals we have for life) to pick a direction, where it presents us with rapids we can use the oars (hard work) to plot a better course.

The next time life takes a turn you don't like and something happens outside of your control take the time to think things through thoroughly before you fight to regain control and ask yourself if it is really worth the fight? Is there a way to use this new turn in your life to influence the overall direction of where you are going? What does real success look like? Can you influence rather than control?

A Little Bit of Fatalism Goes a Long Way

Relinquishing control of your life is not easy. It can be frightening to put your hopes, dreams and ambitions into the hands of forces that you cannot control. There is a very real possibility that things might not turn out as you had envisioned, that life may take you along a path other than what you originally plotted. Yet the realisation that ultimately things are out of your full control can bring you some peace. It can help take the weight off your shoulders, and as a consequence free you to enjoy the ride more and ultimately accomplish even greater things in the end.

The world is a strange place. Just stop to think about it for one moment. In our everyday lives there are hundreds of things that can and possibly should go wrong. Take driving for example. This is one of, if not the most dangerous activity we do every day. Whether in a car, on a motorcycle, or on a bus, driving can kill you. You sit in a metal box that weighs more than a ton and travel at speeds of about 60 miles an hour. If you stop to think about it, it is quite terrifying. One ton of metal traveling 60 miles an hour!

This activity requires a lot of faith. Firstly, you have to have faith in your own (or the driver's) ability to drive the car. Can you handle a one ton steal cage traveling at 60 miles an hour while distractions are all around? The radio, the passengers, the pedestrians on the side of the road and, most shockingly, the massive billboards placed all around you begging you to take your eyes off the road and think about something else. Even if you are not the one doing the driving, you have to have faith. You have to have faith in the driver, you have to believe (contrary to logic in some cases) that nothing is going to happen. Road accidents happen every day and yet you get in a car or a bus and believe that whoever is driving is going to get you to your destination safely. Even if you do trust the driver and you are confident in their skills, you still have to believe that the hundreds of other drivers you will encounter on the roads are good drivers. This, again, is contrary to evidence.

We have all seen on the news, how many people drink and drive or, far more commonly, use their phones and drive. Each one of us has pulled up to a traffic light and seen the person in front of us do something crazy; turn their rear-view mirror so they can comb their hair, pop their head down to pick up something on the floor, hold a phone to their ear, light a cigarette or read a map. Every day we get on the road, we see activities and people that are doing things that could kill us. There are even teenage drivers out there! People who are still in school, girls and boys legally allowed to pilot these death traps. When we stop to think about it, it is very frightening!

Yet, even though we know the risks, we know that we are not fully in control and that ultimately we can only influence the outcome of our journey, we confidently (without thinking about it) get into cars and busses every day. Surely this fact should convince you that there is a bit of fatalism in all of us. We all have the ability to let go, to put our lives in the hands of forces we have no control over and take the journey.

The vast majority of us will drive for over 6 decades without experiencing something serious. We will see things every day that could turn out to be serious yet never do. Because we have been doing this since we were very young, we have gotten used to the situation and we trust that everything will turn out okay.

The lines from a famous Bob Marley song come to mind. He sang:

"Don't worry about a thing,
'cause every little thing is gonna be alright
Singin': Don't worry about a thing,
'cause every little thing is gonna be alright

These lines contain within them both an element of truth and at the same time an element of falsehood. On the one hand everything will be alright. What you are going through and the experiences you have in your life are very similar to the experiences billions of other people are sharing. They all seem to do alright. Your friends and family seem to get along, we seem to find a way to live, a way to eat, find shelter, a person to love, a family to care for. Everything will be okay.

On the other hand everything is not going to be okay. The year Bob Marley recorded this song, in 1977, he was diagnosed with cancer. The year after he released it he died. Yet we all know, even though he died, he did really believe the words and the song has done much to influence the lives of many.

I believe, and this is a belief more than a fact, that the two go together. On the one hand everything will be okay. We will find a way to muddle through this life. If we work hard to influence the direction of our lives, we can make a difference to where we are going and can be successful. There is, for everyone I meet, a very good chance that with a bit of work and direction they will achieve success if their goals are truly worthwhile. On the other hand, life is unpredictable. We never know what is going to happen. Things may go slightly wrong or they may go seriously wrong. Ultimately you cannot fully control life and therefore, beyond trying to influence the outcome, the only appropriate response to life is to let it take its course.

I believe we all need to add a little bit of fatalism to our thinking. Not enough to become defeatists, not enough to give up or even stop trying. Just enough to help us see life for what it is: a game of chance that, with a little bit of luck and hard work, we can be successful at. Sometimes, just sometimes, the correct response to the twists and turns of life, the events that don't go our way, is to accept them, to allow them to be what they are and to acknowledge that failure is simply part of the process.

Enjoy Failing

A number of years ago, while I was still in university, I remember bumping into a lecturer one day. I asked him how he was doing and his response has stuck with me ever since. He said he was doing great. He said he was so busy that he wasn't getting everything done that was required of him. The two statements seemed to me, at that time, to be at odds with each other. How can you be doing great on the one hand and yet not be getting everything done you were supposed to be doing? The university would be upset; his boss should surely be breathing down his neck? It was the end of term, exams needed to be marked, reports needed to be written, end of year statements submitted, university regulations met. Yet he stood before me with a big smile on his face and told me everything was going great.

I asked him what he was going to do, did he think he would get everything done? "No," he said to me, "there is no way everything can be done in time. They could fire me but even then it won't be done."

I had, at that time, known him as a lecturer for just over three years. He was head of distance studies (more than 1000 students) and also a senior professor in the department. More than that, he worked with a number of community groups throughout our city and was even on the national leadership team of a very large charity organisation that funded a large part of the university. He was hardly lazy when he said that everything could not be done in time. He was working really hard, over 50 or 60 hours a week. Yet even with this hard work he knew that everything he needed to get done would not get done and the pressure of having to achieve all these goals did not break him. On the contrary, he seemed to be enjoying the fact that he was failing.

Since my university days, I have kept in contact with him and whenever I return to the university town my wife and I have dinner with him and his wife. He remains very busy. He is, from what I can tell, a very successful person. He set out to change people's lives. To make a difference at "grassroots" level and to teach others who work with "grassroots" organisations. He has achieved his life goals and even though he is beyond the age of retirement he still works tirelessly at what he loves to do. With everything going on, the numerous boards he sits on, the international papers he has written, the students he has taught, the projects he manages, he has had his fair share of success and failures. It seems to me that he treats both with equal joy.

This professor remains an inspiration to me. I have assumed his attitude. While I work very hard, I know that there is no way I will get everything done and I enjoy not getting everything done. By now my poor wife has gotten sick of me saying, with a smile on my face: that's one area I am aiming to fail at. With the realisation that failure does not necessary equate to the loss of success, one is freed from the pressure to be what one is not. One is free to enjoy success and enjoy achieving in areas that are important. When you realise that some failure is not only inevitable but right, you start to have fun failing in those areas.

A line from the famous poem by Kipling comes to mind. In his poem entitled "If" he gives advice to his son on what it means to be a man. Of course, much of what he says can be applied to being a woman as well. He runs through a number of key skills and attitudes he believes a man should be. One that has always stood out to me is the line that goes like this:

"If you can meet with triumph and disaster and treat those two impostors just the same... you'll be a man, my son."

I have saved this poem on my computer and keep it always with me on my handheld device. I often catch myself reading it and asking if "I am a man yet?" I do believe that these words contain an important truth we would do well to heed. We need to treat both our successes and our failures equally. If there has been anything you have learned from this book, I hope it is this message. Failure and success go together, both the product and result of our choices. The one follows the other. Choosing to succeed all the time will ultimately lead to overall failure. Choosing to fail in the right places will ultimately lead to overall success. If we are to be truly successful it is important that we learn not only to aim to fail but to enjoy the failing.

www.ingramcontent.com/pod-product-compliance
Lightning Source LLC
Chambersburg PA
CBHW071506040426
42444CB00008B/1523